Simon Blocker

The Secret of Radiant Christian Living

Other books by Dr. Simon Blocker

PERSONALITY THROUGH PRAYER

WHEN CHRIST TAKES OVER

THE SECRET OF PULPIT POWER

The Secret of Radiant Christian Living

by
SIMON BLOCKER

WM. B. EERDMANS PUBLISHING COMPANY
GRAND RAPIDS, MICHIGAN

Copyright 1957 by
Wm. B. Eerdmans Publishing Company

All rights reserved. No part of this book may be reproduced in any form without permission in writing from the publisher, except brief quotations used in connection with a review in a magazine or newspaper.

First published September 1957

*Library of Congress Catalog
Card Number*: 57-13035

Printed in the United States of America

INTRODUCTION

Thou preparest a table before me in the presence of mine enemies:
Thou hast anointed my head with oil:
My cup runneth over.

So sang the psalmist. Knowing of that table and of that anointing and of the overflowing cup, we desire to show what God has shown, in prayerful hope that it may prove to be light from God to pilgrims heavenward bound.

God's better bread is so tasty and satisfying that impulse comes to pass it around and offer comrades in faith partnership in experienced grace. Flashes come and light is genial, making for brotherliness. What is written is written in benediction; bread of truth being joined in holy wedlock to prayerful wish, in hope that readers may see God's table and God's bounty, and receive anointing and the cup of His salvation.

CONTENTS

	Introduction	5
	Poem: *The Festal Life*	10
1.	THE TRAIL THAT IS ALWAYS NEW	11
	Poem: *I Am Happy, O So Happy*	18
2.	GOD IS HIS OWN INTERPRETER	19
	Poem: *Let Go; Let God*	26
3.	A CHRISTIAN IN WONDERLAND	27
	Poem: *How Wonderful Is Jesus*	34
4.	A CHRISTIAN WHO'S WHO	35
	Poem: *Trust*	42
5.	FACING CRISES WITH CHRIST	43
	Poem: *Hold On to Jesus*	50
6.	COMMANDING GOD'S GIFTS	51
	Poem: *Prayer-Hymn*	60
7.	THE CHURCH UNDER FIRE	61
	Poem: *Mother*	70
8.	THE OLD-FASHIONED MOTHER	71
	POEM: *Face Life with Christ*	78
9.	CHRIST AND CHRISTIAN DESTINY	79
	Poem: *Conscience Speaking*	88
10.	WHAT SHALL I DO WITH JESUS?	89
	Poem: *Creed*	94
11.	THE ONE, ONLY SAVIOUR	95
	Poem: *Prayer for Revival*	102
12.	PARTNERS WITH GOD	103
	Poem: *The Promised Land*	108
13.	SOURCES OF CHRISTIAN JOY	109

The Trail That Is Always New

THE FESTAL LIFE

O God, I thank Thee for the grace
    That keeps me close to Thee;
My life moves on with joyful pace,
    Because Thou lovest me.
I do not mind the cloudy day,
    For Thou, my God, art Light;
I walk with Thee a shining way,
    And find the dark things bright.

O God, I thank Thee for the power
    That makes Thee real and dear;
My life is one glad festal hour,
    Since Thou art always near.
Thy glory, beauty, majesty,
    Are my supreme delight;
My spirit thrills with ecstasy,
    To feel Thy saving might.

O God, I cannot lose with Thee,
    Whatever life may bring;
Almighty love environs me,
    I fear not anything.
All that may come shall work Thy will,
    Thy will, which is my peace;
And even death can mean no ill,
    But only life's increase.

1

THE TRAIL THAT IS ALWAYS NEW

I count all that part of my life lost which I spent not in communion with God, or in doing good.

—JOHN DONNE

WHAT IS THERE to the Christian life? It is to have a life and to live a life which is always increasing, always going from more to more, always becoming richer, fuller, deeper, stronger, and more radiant. It is a steady progress in the appropriation, enjoyment, and use of God's gifts. "The path of the righteous is as the dawning light, that shineth more and more unto the perfect day" (Proverbs 4:18). The Christian life is a trail that is always new.

There is a definite order of development in Christian experience. From strength to strength, from grace to grace, and from glory to glory is the law. "The fruit of the Spirit is love, joy, peace, long-suffering, kindness, goodness, faithfulness, meekness, self-control," and this blessed fruitage comes in successive crops of increase. The tree of life in apocalyptic vision is described as "bearing twelve manner of fruits" or, as the margin says, "twelve crops of fruit, yielding its fruit every month," and the souls of the redeemed are like well-watered gardens where the Spirit of life in Christ Jesus is constantly bringing to fruitage graces and perfections of character.

The truth to get hold of is that the Christian life operates on the same law of increase which lends zest to every sphere of natural quest. That which now goes against the grain will some day be second nature. That which now seems all but impossible will some day be easy. Life will become more and more Christlike, more and more full of love, of joy, of peace, of longsuffering, of kindness, of goodness, of faithfulness, of self-control. God will do more and more for us and in us and through us and make more and more of us as surrender to Jesus Christ becomes more and more complete and we live more fully day by day in the will of God.

The new psychology dotes on the wonders of personality. By voice and pen it summons to fuller self-realization and self-expression. But long before psychology had a name and place among the sciences, God had given to those who fear Him the secret of radiant personality and had served notice on mankind that "the path of the righteous is as the dawning light that shineth more and more unto the perfect day." The source of radiance is character and the ground of character is Jesus Christ. "The path of the righteous" is the Old Testament way of indicating the career and destiny of a Christian. Those who go in for righteousness, who make character their goal, who seek a life which is right with God, become possessed of a life which is God's gift in Christ and which the Holy Spirit creatively sustains and develops.

The world is full of lights, men with candles running up and down the land, loudly proclaiming themselves as bearers and bringers of light. Unconscious of the feebleness of the light that is in them, they call men to follow them, promising to lead into varied realms of light. Every voice seems to be able to command a following, but the promised realms of light are like the mirage in the desert, and darkness remains. Such futile quests give point to God's secret which associates light with character and knows no radiant life apart from fellowship with Him. One may enjoy distinction as an intellectual light, another as a social light, but every child of God is a light of the world, living in growing splendor and shedding an ever brighter luster in the midst of prevailing darkness.

Life is dark without Christ. "The light of the world is Jesus." Brilliant minds, addressing themselves to the problems of life, without looking to Christ for light, form philosophies of pessimism and despair. Average people, caught by the undertow of trouble, flounder about helplessly, tossed to and fro on the sea of life, wondering why things are as they are, unable to see meaning in what happens to them. What seems to one man or nation fundamental is by another individual or nation thrown on the rubbish heap as outworn, outgrown and useless. Forms of government change and new schemes for human betterment prove futile or only partially effective because men plan without Him who is "the light of all our seeing." "The god of this world hath blinded the mind of the unbelieving."

The same God who in the beginning of creation said, "Let there be light," repeats the creative command in every soul which opens to Christ. A real Christian thinks of God as One who has called him "out of darkness into his marvelous light." Whatever vital matter may be the subject of thought, be it God or man or life or sin or sorrow or death or destiny, the natural light that is in us is but a gleam, which in many has become darkness, but the light shed by Christ on it is marvelous. That light needs to be turned on to transform darkness into light and to impress those who walk in it as marvelous. Marvelous light! So much light as to excite marvel. Enough light to make it seem what it is, a miracle of divine bounty.

It is because God's people dwell in such marvelous light that they are exhorted after the manner of the prophet, "Arise, shine: for thy light is come, and the glory of Jehovah is risen upon thee." Every Christian believer may regard that exhortation as addressed to himself. "Seeing it is God, that said, Light shall shine out of darkness, who shined in our hearts, to give the light of the knowledge of the glory of God in the face of Jesus Christ."

Such is our life in Christ, a life of growing light, of increasing luster, of unfolding splendor, "sweeter as the years go by," "glory all the way," a life of constant victory, progressive attainment, enlarging and deepening influence, more and more productive of holy and contagious joy, a life on which the sun never sets, but which shall shine forth at last in the perfected kingdom of the Father. Such is the divine intention, and to this end is the divine provision. "Even so, let your light shine before men; that they may see your good works and glorify your Father who is in heaven."

The Christian life is a trail that is always new only to those who take it seriously. Development of spiritual sensitiveness depends on constancy of consecration and concentration. To do the known will of God is the prime requisite if Christian knowledge is to grow. Prayer must become more and more habitual if the shining life is to move on to perfect day. The steps toward fuller radiance are clearly known. The light of divine truth, enshrined in Scripture, is one step. Neglect of the Word is fatal to progress. The light of God's presence to which prayer admits, is another. Neglecting the place of secret prayer is like pulling down shades and closing shutters. The exercise of the responsiveness of obedience is a step toward growing light. To be a real co-worker with God is to maintain the glow and share in light eternal. A life on which the sun never sets has such distinguishing marks as faith, faithfulness, watchfulness, prayerfulness, devotedness. God deals with us on moral principles. God may be had for the asking, but not without that. He offers Himself freely in Christ, but He will not force His way in. The realm of light is entered, and not forced on one.

There are lights of men and there is the light of God. It is only as life is lighted by the Sun of righteousness that one has within him the radiance that shineth more and more unto the perfect day. To be in Christ is to have the light of life and to be moving steadily on in a career of progressive brightness. "I am the light of the world," says Jesus, "he that followeth me shall not walk in darkness but shall have the light of life."

God Is His Own Interpreter

I AM HAPPY, O SO HAPPY

I am happy, O so happy,
    I am full of joy divine;
Through the love of God, my Father,
    Jesus Christ is fully mine;
God has sent His Holy Spirit
    My dull nature to refine,
And the fire that He has kindled
    Makes my spirit glow and shine.

Jesus keeps my spirit tranquil,
    He abides an honored guest,
And however rough the going,
    He secures that I am blest;
In the turmoil of affliction,
    I enjoy His promised rest,
As I entertain my Saviour
    He sustains me with His best.

Hail, all hail, Thou blessed Saviour,
    Hail to Thee, my God and King;
Glory, glory, world's Redeemer,
    Honor to Thy name I bring;
Linked in worship, saints and angels
    Loud hosannas grandly sing;
Joined with them, eternal praises
    All thy ransomed people sing.

    Halleluiah, Halleluiah,
        Jesus Saviour, Thou art mine
        Glory, Glory, Glory, Glory,
        Be forever, ever Thine.

2

GOD IS HIS OWN INTERPRETER

Faith is to believe, on the word of God, what we do not see, and its reward is to see and enjoy what we believe. —AUGUSTINE

THE VALUE God places on faith goes far to clear up the mystery of suffering. God prizes faith so highly that He rewards it thirty, sixty, and a hundredfold. A little faith can remove a mountain of difficulties. A strong faith sees vast opportunity in most trying situations and can speak of them as Paul did concerning his work in Ephesus, "for a great door and effectual is opened unto me, and there are many adversaries." Moreover, a great faith has the sense of having "always all sufficiency for all things" and that this sufficiency is of God. So it is that God looks for faith, labors to inspire it, rewards it liberally, is pleased with it, nourishes it by all the methods of His providence, and graciously increases it by every means at His command.

God looks with interest on all good deeds of men. God loves to see a great faith in action. God loves to exhibit those who have great faith and who are out and out for God at all times, under all circumstances, and at all costs. Next to that, God loves to see and exhibit people who with little faith are removing mountains and casting them into the sea. He who made all worlds and sent them spinning into space created man in His own image. When man with God's image in him musters enough faith to hurl a mountain into the sea, it gives God a degree of pleasure second only to the pleasure it gives Him to see a man with faith so strong that "every valley is exalted, every mountain and hill made low, the uneven made level, and the rough places a plain."

The dark side of life gives faith its chance. "Without faith it is impossible to please God." The mountains are there in order that man may master mountains. God so values faith that by His decree a mere mustard-seed supply of it enables one to go into the business of removing mountains. If faith is full-orbed, the believer rides on top of all circumstances. "He that sitteth in the heavens" laughs when His believing people do a bit of mountain hurling or when by faith they so rise in spiritual stature as to take God's view of things before whom mountains and valleys alike are highways.

It may still be God's pastime in new-born worlds to make mountains or to hurl them into seas. Here on earth God is in the business of growing souls. God is at work fashioning character according to the pattern of the man Christ Jesus. God is engaged in making human nature partaker of the divine nature. He is ushering in His imperishable kingdom of which Jesus Christ is the foundation and chief cornerstone. Man gets in on all this by faith. He needs faith to see what God is about. He needs faith to appropriate what God wants him to have. He needs more and more faith to measure up to what God has in store for him. Since man is naturally inclined to make the house of life of cards and to set it up on sand, inevitable collapse is God's call to see and accept and go in for a house not made with hands, and grounded on the Rock of Ages.

God wants to be trusted. God deserves to be trusted. God insists on being trusted. God does everything possible to win a person's trust. God has done so much to get souls to trust Him that it seems to many too good to be true. God became man in order that man might trust Him. When a man really and fully trusts God like the patriarch Job did, when a man is so sure of God that he can say, "Though he slay me, yet will I trust him," God points with pride to that man saying, "Hast thou considered my servant Job?"

The reason God was so pleased with Jesus was that Jesus as a believing man trusted God with unbroken and complete faith. It is a lifelong study to search out the wonder of the faith of Jesus. The hidden years at Nazareth were a stupendous triumph of faith. Think of a young man like Jesus waiting thirty years to get started on his real work! Our gifted children are heard over the air long before they know what it is all about. They are seen on the screen and earn huge sums before they come to their teen age. Jesus waited thirty years to begin, waited and trusted, waited because he believed God.

Jesus kept on trusting God when the time to begin His public ministry had begun. What a battle for faith was won when Jesus was "led of the Spirit into the wilderness to be tempted of the devil"! Jesus trusted God so fully that He said "No" to every temptation and never swerved a hair's breadth from perfect obedience. Jesus trusted God every step of the way in His public ministry, careful to observe the appointed hour, neither running ahead nor lagging behind in the way of self-giving. Jesus trusted God when the world He had come to redeem nailed Him to the Cross. Three short years had to suffice to bring His work to its redemptive finish. He was but thirty-three when in faith He climbed up Calvary. The seven sayings from the Cross begin and end with the name "Father": "Father, forgive them; for they know not what they do." "Father, into thy hands I commend my spirit." Even when Jesus felt forsaken of God He kept trusting God. The personal possessive is found in the cry of dereliction. Jesus cried, "My God, my God, why hast Thou forsaken me?" What faith, to be able still to say "my," to feel bereft of God and yet cry to Him as possessing Him! "Wherefore also God highly exalted him."

If a man believes God in God's estimate of His son, if he believes that "in none other is there salvation," if he believes God so perfectly that he places his trust absolutely in Jesus Christ as Saviour and Lord, God gives such a man salvation on the spot. God gives such a believing man a new birth of freedom. Be the man what he may, though like Peter he be rough, rude, profane, cowardly and false, God puts a new song in that man's heart, causing him to sing, "Blessed be the God and Father of our Lord Jesus Christ, who according to his great mercy begat us again unto a living hope by the resurrection of Jesus Christ from the dead, unto an inheritance incorruptible and undefiled, and that fadeth not away, reserved in heaven for you, who by the power of God are guarded through faith unto a salvation ready to be revealed in the last time."

Reserved in heaven as the salvation is and ready as it is to be revealed "in the last time" God gives a believing man, whose trust is in Christ, the germ and principle and power of salvation for immediate possession, so that the predicted "last time" seems to be here already, so great is the believer's rejoicing in what God is doing for his soul. The apostle John had a way of saying "it is the last hour." No wonder! It seemed to himself that he had all of God's salvation. His cup was constantly running over. Filled as he was unto all the fullness of God, what more could there be in reserve? Full of God as he was, the dear old saint did not fail to look forward to seeing face to face. Well he knew that to have all you can hold of Christ's salvation is not the measure of what God has in mind to give. A believing heart gets bigger and bigger and is thus made ready for the salvation "ready to be revealed in the last time." The power of God is pledged, "according to his great mercy" to guard every believer's salvation. God will see to it that the believer and his salvation get and stay together, in union forever, moving in holy wedlock to God's purposed goal.

Faith pleases God. Faith is what God counts precious in a life. God so prizes faith that when a heart is full of it, God loves to exhibit it, to show that it is real. God loves to strengthen faith. God will permit circumstances which put believers to grief. God permits this in hope that their faith will stand out and grow and be seen to belong to the very texture of the soul. God has in mind to make something great of every Christian life.

We are "justified by faith." We are "saved by grace through faith." Justified as we are by faith, saved as we are by grace through faith and happy as we are in the love of Jesus, God wants to go on with us, is determined to go on with us in order to make our faith a great faith, a faith that trusts God in the dark, a faith that sees eye to eye with God and does the impossible. God leads from faith to faith, giving cause for rejoicing, yet allowing to be put to grief by "manifold trials," but always helping to hold out and to hold on, and to hold up a firm — even if weather-beaten and battle-scarred — front to every wind that blows.

God's best comes into life in the way of faith. Our best comes out in a life of faith. Trials rightly borne relieve us of hindrances. "That the proof of your faith, being more precious than gold that perisheth though it is proved by fire, may be found unto praise and glory and honor at the revelation of Jesus Christ" (I Peter 1:7). The fire that tries burns up dross, such dross as self-confidence, self-righteousness, pride, censoriousness, selfishness, covetousness, insensitiveness.

It must also be remembered that "no man liveth unto himself." God uses the faith of one to inspire others to believe. Much as God plans to do for one who trusts, God lures others to look at one who trusts in hope that the example he sets of enduring faith and of comfort in affliction may hearten them to venture all on God in Christ.

It comes to this that to be tried by fire is proof that God is at work in one for his own and other's good. There should be no doubt, no wavering, no protests, no rebellion. Life may seem to be just one blow after another, but the life of faith will yet prove to be unto "praise and glory and honor." God means well with us. It is not God's aim to disappoint, to thwart, to take the joy out of life. God applies Himself to the needs of every believer and acts in such a manner that what it is in us to become shall be brought out. God keeps a firm hand on circumstances. He will see one through to a joyous end. If God withdrew and left one to his own devices, he might well despair. But with God as our God, and such a God as He is, *nihil desperandum* (nothing is to be despaired of). "Hope thou in God, for I shall yet praise him, who is the help of my countenance, and my God."

A Christian in Wonderland

LET GO; LET GOD

I put my trust in God,
He makes His purpose known;
I look to Him for light,
The way is clearly shown.

He operates my life,
To bring it to its best:
He gives me what it takes,
To meet the fiery test.

He knows the way I feel,
And what I have to bear;
He makes me through life's all,
The object of His care.

'Tis grandeur when a man,
His spirit overawed,
Discovers in distress,
That he is loved of God.

The Saviour is on hand,
The Holy Spirit, too;
The Triune God is pledged,
To see a Christian through.

To live can be superb,
However rough the road,
When God conducts you, safe,
To His divine abode.

3

A CHRISTIAN IN WONDERLAND

God — This is one of the names which we give to that eternal, infinite, and incomprehensible being, the creator of all things, who preserves and governs everything by his almighty power and wisdom, and who is the only object of our worship. —Cruden

WHEN ONE REALLY GETS to know God he will be moved to worship and adoration. To be thus moved to worship and adoration does not require a full understanding of all God's ways with men. It is enough to get the general drift of what God is like and what He is about. We need only to find out that God is trustworthy, that His purpose is beneficent, that His plans are efficient, and that His resources are adequate. Insight into God's heart is enough for peace and joy. "The trusting heart goes singing."

Writing to Roman Christians, Paul takes up the problem of Jewish unbelief. Looking into this great mystery, he comes, as it were, face to face with God. No matter how far back in history he goes, he finds God present with purpose to redeem and save. He discovers that God, in His desire to bring humanity to the highest plane of living, refuses to be thwarted. God is seen to be sovereign. He keeps things in hand. He rules and overrules. He brings good out of evil. He makes the wrath of man to praise Him and the remainder of wrath He restrains.

God will not step aside and let things go as they will. His redemptive interest in mankind is a permanent feature of His character. His redeeming activity in the world is continuous. His resources are inexhaustible. Paul sees that God means to have his way and that God's way is our peace. Like a divine Potter God is busy with human clay. He will make of it what He pleases. He will do the best He can with it. He does not work with it in order to destroy it. He has some sort of vessel in mind. What He has in mind will be to the praise of the glory of His grace. No matter what may prove at last to be the destiny of any human being, that actual destiny will proclaim that God is love.

It was revealed to Paul and it became Paul's insight what God is like and what God is about. In trying to realize the revelation and share the insight, we must try to visualize the colossal power of sin in the world and then ask what kind of a God will be equal to the situation. The effort will advance us along the road on which Paul received his salvation and insight.

Think of the stupendous forces of evil resident in human nature and operative in the world. Minorities embody ideals in national life calculated to produce a godless civilization and to found governments on absolute atheism. The futility of legislation, however noble, is patent to the world when such legislation runs athwart unredeemed desire. From certain angles of vision it seems as if actual tendencies in the general life of the world are moving society to the brink of destruction. Strains of pessimism are very pronounced in the discussions and prophecies of scientific writers.

Think of the situation in this way. Imagine yourself appointed to arrest the fatal drift of human society. Conceive of yourself as charged to bring moral transformation to the world. Try to feel it laid upon you to change human nature, to cleanse its pollution, to purify desire, to empower the will in the direction of nobler living. Would not anyone sink in despair before such a commission?

Put yourself in God's place. Here is the world with the vast power of sin universally operative. Everywhere is disobedience, protest, rebellion, lustful living, greedy self-seeking, secular idealism, vulgar egoism. In the desire to be free mankind is ever forging new chains for itself. Such is the world as it lies open to God's gaze. Such is the world, but it is not only or all such. God has not kept aloof. He has pitted against the power of sin the much more abounding power of His redeeming grace. If sin is universal, so is God. Paul came to see that the God who is sovereign is a redeeming God. He is not indifferent to what is going on. He does not stand idly by. He has been doing something about the sin of the world from the very beginning. God concentrated His redemptive effort on one people, all the while keeping an eye on the whole world, giving to one people what He meant the whole world to have. When the one people as a whole rejected what God offered, God turned to the whole world with it, always keeping His eye on the one people, intent to get them to accept it, too, since they saw from others who had it what they themselves were missing.

Paul came to see that God evidently wanted every human being to be saved. He came to see that God had been actively related to mankind in order to free it "from the law of sin and death" and to bring it "under the law of the Spirit of life in Christ Jesus." He came to see that where life was missing what God had provided, it was due to unbelief. Unwillingness to receive salvation as a gift destroys the moral lights of the soul, and efforts at working out a man-made salvation prove futile. Paul was baffled by Jewish unbelief, but he learned that God is not to be charged with it. God's goodness is manifest in providing a way of salvation, a way which is the only possible way. God's severity is manifest in that those fall who refuse to walk in God's way. No one is to blame for the fall of those who fall except those who fall, seeing God has opened a way in which His uttermost salvation is available for all.

What Paul saw of God filled him with rapture: "O the depth of the riches both of the wisdom and the knowledge of God! How unsearchable are his judgments and his ways past finding out" (Romans 11:33). God does as He pleases, but it is His pleasure to save. God is sovereign. If he were not sovereign sin would prevail until it had brought mankind to destruction: both temporal, spiritual, and eternal. God is sovereign and therefore there is a church militant destined to be a church triumphant. That God is sovereign guarantees a growing Kingdom of God and a time when Jesus Christ shall be King of kings. It takes a sovereign God to handle the world situation brought about by sin.

Much remains dark, but it is a great light to know where God stands. His character is redemptive. His interest in mankind is redemptive. His activity in the world all down the ages is redemptive. The host of the redeemed in this and in the heavenly sphere is prophetic of the vast redemptive victory which God is achieving. Paul received a view of it which filled his heart with adoring praise. God was breaking the power of reigning sin. He was taking the burden of guilt from the conscience and cleansing its defilement. He was bringing moral repair and renewal to lives which sin had broken. He was recreating human character, making all things new for people, in producing a life which was of divine workmanship. He had brought into life through Christ a spirit of regeneration.

God is always carrying out his saving purpose. Although thwarted by the responsible choice of moral freedom, God is never defeated. He is an eternally persistent Redeemer. He never gives up. His resources are varied and inexhaustible. There is much we crave to know which abides a mystery. But we can be sure of God. He is merciful. He is mighty. He is wise. He delights to save. He is at work undoing the mischief of sin. In Christ He has brought life and immortality to light. We do not even have to fear death. Nothing can separate from the love of God which is in Christ Jesus our Lord. Life is a great separator and so is death. But when God saves we are safe from these and all other separators.

The thing to remember is that God makes possible for man such insight into His ineffable nature, such experience of His reality and goodness, such realization of His grace and glory, such satisfaction with His being, such appreciation of His spiritual gifts, such appropriation of His own true divine life, that personality becomes radiant, life is filled with rapture, and inspiration is felt to perpetual praise. God is ready to lead the seeking and trusting heart into the wonderland of divine communion. His fellowship with man in love can be a matter of personal experience. Human nature is capable of being so sensitized that God becomes a living reality, and realization of what He is inspires grateful worship and adoration. Once see and know God as He is, once glimpse His saving presence, His saving power and wisdom operative in human life, and the reaction of the spirit of man can only be grateful recognition and adoring wonder.

A Christian Who's Who

HOW WONDERFUL IS JESUS

How wonderful is Jesus enthroned at God's right hand,
With glory crowned and honor, and worthy to command;
All nations shall obey Him and own His righteous sway,
His love at last shall conquer and bring the crowning day.

How wonderful is Jesus enthroned within my heart,
What thrills of holy rapture through my whole being start;
He gives the life abundant, my every want supplies,
With sovereign grace and glory my spirit satisfies.

How wonderful is Jesus enthroned in other lives,
How great the change effected in whom His spirit thrives;
A beauty rests upon them, the beauty of the Lord,
A light, a fire, a fragrance is in their nature stored.

How wonderful is Jesus wherever else enthroned,
Preeminent as Saviour whose death for sin atoned;
Our speech shall tell the story, our songs proclaim the praise
Of Jesus, blessed Jesus, whose wonders still amaze.

4

A CHRISTIAN WHO'S WHO

Newton, Pascal, Bossuet, Racine, Fenelon, that is to say some of the most enlightening men on earth, in the most philosophical of all ages, have been believers in Jesus Christ; and the great Condé, when dying, repeated these noble words, "Yes, I shall see God as he is, face to face." —VAUVENARGUES

To KNOW MEN after the flesh is to estimate them according to their station and circumstances in this present world. It is to size them up according to blood-relationships, financial and social standing, and eminence in any field of endeavor. To know men in such a sense usually involves an appraisal of worth or its opposite and issues in a verdict of acceptance or ostracism. From this standpoint, one man is worth millions and another is not worth a cent; one is regarded as "the class," another as a social nobody; one is the pride of intellectual circles, another simply does not belong.

To know oneself after the flesh is to value oneself according to current standards of judgment. So valued, one is rich, learned, elite, or gifted; another is poor, ignorant, common, or a good-for-nothing. To know oneself thus is to adopt the natural view of self, to harbor an inferiority or superiority complex, to put ourselves where the world says we belong or where we think we belong.

"Wherefore we henceforth know no man after the flesh; even though we have known Christ after the flesh, yet now we know Him so no more" — 2 Corinthians 5:16.

To know Christ after the flesh is to know Him as a man among men, a member of the human race, a Jew of Palestine, the carpenter of Nazareth, a healer and teacher who came to an untimely end by crucifixion, a man of poverty whose gracious teachings and kindly deeds terminated in ignominious death, but the knowledge of whom by those who came within the charm of His life was regarded as a distinguishing asset after He was gone. So known, Christ is appraised as a man and no more than a man, His earthly rank and fortune setting limits to His significance.

It is perhaps natural that people should be classified. Numerous labels assign each individual to his proper human sphere. The letters of the alphabet are joined in varied wedlock to register degrees of attainment in this or that domain of knowledge and often these degrees are honorary, conferring upon the recipient a classification to which he is regarded as entitled, though unearned in the regular way.

The extent of the classification of people is almost boundless, registering endless variety in condition, circumstances and attainment. There are leaders and the masses, rich and poor, learned and ignorant, socially elect and social nobodies, and so on. The tendency is to judge a man's worth and significance by the class to which he is assigned.

Those who are relegated to a class regarded as inferior may find themselves ambitious to escape to a better class. The result is a scramble to achieve a superior classification. Success in the effort begets pride, with accompanying contempt for those who do not make the grade. Those who are less ambitious may accept their lot as final and slink down into discouraged indifference.

Christianity introduces a revised estimate. It spreads an atmosphere of fresh appreciation over our world. It inspires appraisal from the standpoint of God's redeeming purpose in Christ. It reveals that every human being is dear to God and has relation to a spiritual world order of far greater importance than his standing in the natural order. Whatever a man's earthly lot, he is a potential saint, he is a man whom Christ died to redeem. His call and destiny is to be a member of the imperishable kingdom of God, a citizen of that heavenly commonwealth of which Jesus Christ is the founder.

God has comprehended all men under the one classification of sinner, a classification absolutely to the point, and He has had mercy upon all men so classified, bringing life and immortality to light through the Gospel, opening to each and all a way into righteousness and eternal blessedness as children of God. However undistinguished a man's earthly lot, if he knows Jesus Christ, the eternal Son of God, as his Saviour and Lord, his life is changed with an unseen glory, ready to be revealed in due time. However exalted a man's station in the present world order, if he is not in Christ his life is charged with an unseen shame, ready to be revealed in the final appraisal.

Human standards of appraisal and man's classification of his fellow-men may be natural and useful up to a point, but in God's sight they constitute the great irrelevance. The brotherhood of man is an idea and fact which the world owes to the religion of the Bible. This brotherhood reposes on no identity of earthly rank or fortune, but is constituted by his being created in God's image and being redeemed by Christ the Saviour. The universal need of Christ's salvation reduces every man to a common level in God's sight and the universal redemption provided in Christ lifts every man to the same high pinnacle of spiritual possibility.

High classification in the appraisal of mankind involves grave perils. The temptation is to look down instead of up, and looking down makes one dizzy with pride, and "pride cometh before a fall." The only safe course is to look up and measure human attainment and standing by God's intention. The self-satisfied can do his own cross-examining of himself. Is there anything in the way of forgiveness needed? Is there any sense of guilt weighing down on his complacent spirit? Anything evil in the nature to be rooted out? Any fly in the ointment of his eminence? Is there no bitter ingredient in life's cup which no merely human specific can sweeten? Any shred of darkness, calling for light? Any gnawing emptiness in fancied fulness? Any longing for unattained completeness? Any fear of death or craving to outwit it? Any feeling of going downhill and facing impending disaster? Honest inquiry, detached from the blinding forces of pride, leads to quick discovery of needs which only Christ is competent to meet. What are riches or learning or eminence or any other natural goal of man's quest for pilgrims who have here no continuing city? Why value too highly what must be left behind and is at any rate impertinent to the basic fabric of the soul?

The true estimate of man is grounded on the knowledge of the spiritual structure of personality and the apprehension of its relation to a spiritual world order. Christ has the key to the eternal kingdom of God. He has opened it to all believers. And every man is a possible believer in his own incompetence and the qualified Saviour. The importance of every human being arises from the fact that God has redeemed him in Christ and confronted him with the possibility of eternal glory. The man who is not worth a penny is thus of immeasurable worth as a potential child of God and an heir of a vast spiritual inheritance. The man with millions gets his value not from the millions but from his possible completeness in Christ.

God's purpose in Christ is a universal spiritual aristocracy, a full realization of the apostolic slogan, "every man perfect in Christ Jesus." It is an aristocracy of character, of the spirit of sonship to God, and of blessedness in the consciousness of the love of our heavenly Father. Earthly discriminations between men are beside the mark. Human classifications are futile. However defaced the stamp of Deity on human nature, the uttermost derelict shares it with the most virtuous product of civilization and in both its restoration in Christ is possible. That faded stamp of Deity gives every man his worth in God's sight. When a man gets to see what a shining reality that corroded image is destined to become, if Christ gets a chance at him, he will no longer regard appraisals of men as true or final, but will estimate all men in the light of their unseen and eternal glory in Christ.

Before Paul became a Christian he might have laid just claim to a place in the "Who's Who" of his day. His was a mighty intellect and he was entitled by training and station to belong to the circle of the distinguished. But when God revealed Christ in him and he had taken time to think things through, he realized that the true worth of man lies in what God has purposed to make of him. His capability of becoming a new man in Christ is his regal asset. Environed as a man is by a spiritual world order and sought of God in a divine crusade of redemption, his having a place in the seeking and saving grace of Christ lends to him a significance and value which all men should honor. Classification according to physical descent or material condition may place him too high or too low. Whatever the status according to the standards of human judgment, it is an injustice to assign one to this or that category, seeing that God's standard — recognizing a universal abasement — acknowledges the redeemableness of all. Paul thus looked at all men in the light of God's purpose and Christ's redeeming death. He lost sight of externals and saw in every man the brother for whom Christ died.

To know men after the flesh, to estimate them by what they have or lack in a financial, social, or intellectual way, is to promote the class spirit and to erect barriers between lives fundamentally linked in commonalty of need and privilege.

By unwarranted appraisal of men in terms of blood or condition, social asperities multiply, human life is seduced and reduced to competitive rigor, and many a crime against brotherly fellowship perpetrated. No man has ever risen in resurrection glory from death except Christ, and since it is His will to share with all the benefits of His vicarious achievement, it ill becomes any to frown on another because of irrelevant differences. In a material and physical way, "the paths of glory lead but to the grave" and mortal man approaches the moment when his miseries are great upon him. In view of the common weakness and humiliation confronting everyone and the common redemption which claims all for God and eternal blessedness, the fitting attitude is one of grateful reception of Christ, eager presentation of Him to those who still fail of their eternal inheritance, and the honoring of all men as precious in God's sight.

Facing Crises with Christ

TRUST

Oft in the joy of strong deliverance
God's providence is clearly manifest;
I see in the rich content of that hour
Wisdom and power and love divine expressed.
Why then not trust that these still operate
In times of unexplained adversity;
That through the mystery of pain and tears
The same sweet Sovereign love is holding me?

5

FACING CRISES WITH CHRIST

Difficulties are God's errands; and when we are sent upon them we should esteem it a proof of God's confidence — as a compliment from him.

—H. W. BEECHER

EVER SINCE Paul's day the word "Crete" has stood for more than an island in the Mediterranean. It has stood for the rough side of life. It has stood for a hard human lot. It has stood for hateful and all but unbearable circumstances. It has stood for predicaments where we pray, "Father, if it be possible, let this cup pass." It has stood for heart-rending experiences when it has been natural to cry, "My God, my God, why hast thou forsaken me?" The word "Crete" has become an elastic synonym for adversity of every degree and description.

Every one who knew his geography in Paul's day knew that Crete was a large island and thickly populated. The length of it was 270 Roman miles. It was 50 miles across at the broadest point. The coastal line was 589 miles. Crete could boast of one hundred famous cities.

Long before John R. Mott wrote his famous book, *The Evangelization of the World in this Generation,* Paul had the substance of that title for his slogan. Spent as the great apostle was with missionary labors and travels, he eyed Crete with holy passion, judging that the evangelization of that island would be a fitting climax of his missionary career.

Paul came across a statement of a native Cretan to this effect, "The Cretans are always liars, evil beasts, idle gluttons." That settled it for him. He was soon in Crete. He found the testimony true. The Cretans were such liars that a new verb for lying had been formed out of the noun "Crete." To "cretize" meant to lie. So avaricious and unscrupulous were the Cretans that "to play the Cretan against a Cretan" meant "to play a trick on a trickster." The more Paul saw of current Cretan corruption, the more he said, "Woe is me if I preach not the gospel" in Crete. Spent as he was, he made the rounds of the most famous of the famous cities, pitting the Gospel against their infamy and finding it once again "the power of God unto salvation." The mission to Crete became a march to victory over all obstacles. Sinners were converted and Christian churches sprang into being. Paul's slogan kept him on the move. Presently, he was out of Crete, having fulfilled a glorious ministry and leaving Titus, a younger Christian disciple of his, to develop overseers and consolidate the work.

Titus was not yet attuned to the challenge of the difficult. It seemed to him useless to stay in Crete. What could he hope to do among such sordid people? He had never seen such lawlessness and disorder. He probably wrote to Paul of his desire to get out of Crete. He doubtless gave Paul plenty of gruesome details in support of his appeal to be permitted to quit Crete.

Paul's answer was, "For this cause left I thee in Crete that thou shouldest set in order the things that are wanting." Paul left Titus in Crete for the very reason Titus gave for wanting to get out. We are reminded of something which was said at college over thirty years ago. The speaker was the late Dr. Wilbur F. Crafts of the International Reform Bureau at Washington, D. C. The gist of his remarks to the student body was summed up in four statements: (1) The world was originally right side up. (2) The world is now upside down. (3) The world must be turned right side up again. (4) And we are the chaps to do it. That is what Paul meant to say to Titus. The Christian task is set by what's wrong with the world. It is as if Paul wrote, "Dear Titus, all you say about Crete is true. Things are even worse than you say. But that is no reason for giving up and getting out. There is work for Christ to be done, work which is all but impossible. I left you there to do it, not in your strength, but with the help of God. It will be the making of you to stay in Crete and see it through."

Titus did as Paul said. He found that when a man works for God in a hard place, God works with him and in him. He entered by faith and obedience into a more radiant and efficient life. He discovered that his work was not fruitless. Things began to happen. Weak Christians became strong. Bad men became good. Crete was a terrible place, but it became a better place through the work of Titus. Titus had his cross. His cross was Crete. But he became a better man by bearing his cross and doing his bit and his best for Crete. He was either abroad in spiritual quest among the cities of Crete or on his knees before God praying for strength and for souls.

Can anyone doubt that Titus later thanked Paul for making him stay in Crete? Titus came to see that Crete had been a supreme opportunity. His stay there had led to the richest experiences of his life. He "climbed the steep ascent of heaven through peril, toil, and pain." God used him to consolidate work which Paul had started. God used Crete as a means of grace for Titus.

Such is life. Opposition is opportunity to one who lives in the will of God. Foes will be seen at last to have been friends of our deepest well-being. The wonder-working God makes even the wrath of man to praise Him. The wrath of man becomes the occasion of praise to God when God's people come to see how God has made all things to work together for good in their Christian life and warfare. God will not allow the wrath of man to go beyond the point where praises to God and blessing for His obedient people can be gotten out of it. "The remainder of wrath," the useless part of it as far as divine purpose is concerned, God restrains. In the sphere of Christian faith and obedience, life is a fight, but it is a good fight. We incline to look for a way out. God is much more apt to give us power to work our way through. We may, like Elisha's servant, be more in need of opened eyes than of a quick get-away (II Kings 6:15-17).

What we are up against is given as raw material for splendid achievement. A tight place is meant to be a field of victory. The reality of Christian faith and life is tested by the way we react to trying situations. To fight a good fight is in itself a triumph. When one finds it in him "to endure hardness as a good soldier of Jesus Christ" victory already perches on his banner. Crete is a tough place but Crete has possibilities. To see what God wants done, to believe in the power of Christ to make bad men good, and to meet the challenge of hostile circumstances with consecration and determination is really to move on "from strength to strength, from grace to grace, and from glory to glory."

Make no mistake in this matter! When it is said that Christ is "able to save to the uttermost" it means that He is equal to every situation in which a Christian may find himself. It not only means that the worst sinner may be saved, but that the most sorely tried Christian may win out right where he is. What would be the use of going elsewhere if Christ cannot give victory where we are?

Every missionary of the Cross is in Crete and has his Crete. So has every minister. If there are country parsons who sigh for the city, there are also city parsons who sigh for the country. Church institutions and agencies are all in Crete and have their Crete. Every home and every individual is in Crete and has a Crete. Whatever or wherever this Crete, this crisis of individual or institution is, there "the kingdom and the power and the glory" belong to Christ and golden possibilities challenge faith and obedience.

No use running away from Crete. After all, "one with God is a majority." O my soul, plead for Christ's uttermost salvation in Crete. Believe and claim the promises. Walk humbly with God. Do not run ahead of God. Learn to follow. This be your prayer: "Keep back thy servant also from presumptuous sins; let them not have dominion over me." Face Crete with Christ. Remember that God's Word shall not return unto Him void. "Void," say we. "Not void," says God. Remember that they who "sow in tears shall reap in joy." Remember that the Gospel is "the power of God unto salvation" and that we get our word "dynamite" out of the Greek word for power.

Use the dynamite of God in Crete. Keep that dynamite in stock. We are meant to win. We have got to win. We are going to win. We can do all things in Christ who gives us strength. "O, for a faith that will not shrink!"

"My God, my God, why hast thou left me in Crete?"

"For this cause left I thee in Crete, that thou shouldest set in order the things that are wanting."

Commanding God's Gifts

HOLD ON TO JESUS

Hold on to Jesus, doubt His mercy never,
He died upon the Cross for sin and guilt;
Hold on to Jesus, trust His love forever,
His blood in costly sacrifice was spilt.

Hold on to Jesus, He alone is Saviour
He freely pardons all who seek His grace;
His Spirit rescues from corrupt behavior,
And fits the soul to see His blessed face.

Hold on to Jesus, in His Word confiding,
The weakest gains and holds sure standing ground;
By faith and deed in His sweet love abiding,
The far horizons of the soul are found.

Hold on to Jesus in the way appointed,
By roughest road He gained the highest goal;
Keep close to Christ and pray for eyes anointed,
To see how safe and kind is His control.

Hold on to Jesus, bright will be the morrow,
No matter what the burden of today;
Lean hard on Christ, firm resolution borrow,
To wait fair issue of the cross-crowned way.

Hold on to Jesus, loving each the other,
And make the desert blossom like the rose;
Where Christ is King and every man a brother,
The joys of Kingdom come replace earth's woes.

Hold on to Jesus, Christian, hold on;
Hold on to Jesus, the crowning day will dawn.

6

COMMANDING GOD'S GIFTS

Prayer is a sincere, sensible, affectionate pouring out of the soul to God, through Christ, in the strength and assistance of the Spirit, for such things as God has promised. —BUNYAN

A BEAUTIFUL STORY tells of two women who were very dear friends. They exchanged presents at the Christmas season and found delight in serving each other with kindly deeds. Everything that one did for the other represented careful and loving thought.

It was Christmas morning. One of these women might have been seen in evident bewilderment with an opened package before her. It was a gift from her bosom friend, a gift consisting of a key with an explanatory letter. The letter told that the key was to the sender's house, that a room was perpetually ready for the recipient of the key, that she might avail herself at any time of the hospitality of the home to which she held the key.

Bewilderment soon gave way to realization. The more the gift was thought on the more significant it seemed. It became to the recipient the symbol of deepest love, of absolute trust, of desire for fellowship. The key to the house of her friend became to this woman the very choicest gift her friend could have given.

Not otherwise does Jesus treat His friends. He tells them on what terms they may secure the key to His treasure-house and live a life where the gifts of God shall be at their command. "If ye abide in me, and my words abide in you, ye shall ask what ye will, and it shall be done unto you."

In the Acts of the Apostles is the story of one Simon the Sorcerer who by his sorcery had gotten a reputation for being some great one. One day Peter and John came into town preaching the Gospel. Many believed and Simon the Sorcerer saw something that startled him. He saw Peter and John laying hands on the heads of new believers and praying, and behold, these new believers received the Holy Spirit. When Simon the Sorcerer saw this he made his way to Peter and John and offered them money, saying, "Give me also this power, that on whomsoever I lay my hands, he may receive the Holy Spirit." But he was swiftly rebuked and informed that the spirit he had shown was utterly alien to the nature of the Christian life. Spiritual power is not a commodity which can be bought and sold in open market. It is a gift of God and available only for those who are fully surrendered to Jesus Christ.

The fact should commend itself to every person of intelligence that God deals with His people on moral principles. God plays no favorites but offers to all the possession and use of spiritual power on condition of abiding in Christ and being dominated by His teachings. God thinks so highly of His Son that He is ready to give the key to His treasure-house to anyone who adopts the divine estimate and allows Jesus full sway in his life.

In the great promise of Jesus attention is apt to fasten on the words, "Ask whatsoever ye will, and it shall be done unto you." Only God knows how many people have prayed for something they wanted, pleading this promise as a reason why their request should be granted, and because they failed to get what they asked have given up praying, protesting that there is no good in it! Many tragic volumes could be written recording disappointment in prayer and subsequent experiences of bitterness and unbelief. If the truth were told, many would divulge that they have a secret grudge against God because of failure to get what they feel they asked so sincerely and wanted so passionately. Or, at any rate, there is a permanent hidden perplexity which they never expect to have cleared up in this world, some insistent interrogation in this matter of prayer which they would like to have God Himself answer. Perhaps there is a buried grief because the thing asked and apparently denied was the life of one more precious than rubies and dearer than their own life; a grief which now and again rises to the surface, so that even after the lapse of years it is felt as keenly as ever and we and it are linked inseparably. Whatever of good life may yet hold, nothing can ever take the place of what was lost or denied and nothing, however desirable, can possibly be to us what it would have been if that unanswered prayer had been answered. Thus we reason, confirming the Scripture that every heart knoweth its own bitterness.

Who that has had an inner life with God and personal dealings with Him in some matter of vital concern has not been shocked to discover something akin to a grudge against God assuming shape and strength? We knew it to be a sin and not God's due and hastened to confess, only to find, perhaps, that the perplexity and grief remained as comrades on the way. We try to keep them in abeyance until such time as we shall see face to face.

> Not now, but in the coming years,
> It may be in the better land,
> We'll read the meaning of our tears,
> And there, sometime, we'll understand.

It is important to recall that the large promise of Jesus is not made without qualification, is not made to everybody indiscriminately, and does not include everything that we may feel inclined to regard as included. But when every allowance has been made, there is a breadth and a wealth in the promise which should lure the soul to get within the sweep of it. It is evidently Jesus' purpose to promise big things to His followers, to put them in the way of gaining great power and having vast resources. But the conditions as clearly show that He is seeking to lure them to certain heights of character and to a quality of motive and service which shall reveal the reality of their union with Him in His life and work. This life-union with Christ is the immediate object of Jesus' promise.

"If ye abide in me, and my words abide in you, ask whatsoever ye will, and it shall be done unto you." To abide in Christ is "to consent with our whole soul to His being our life, to reckon upon Him to inspire us in all that goes to make up life, and then to give up everything most absolutely for Him to rule and work in us." "It is the rest of the full assurance that He does, each moment, work in us what we are to be, and so enables us to maintain that perfect surrender, in which He is free to do all His will." So wrote the saintly Andrew Murray. And now let another saint tell us what is meant by Christ's words abiding in us, "It means the whole of the conscious nature of a man being, so to speak, saturated with Christ's words; his desires, his understanding, his affections, his will, all being steeped in these great truths which the Master spoke."

Here we have a description of life according to God's plan, a life to which Christ is all, which feeds on Christ and reproduces Him, which is constantly being molded by every word that comes from the mouth of the Son of God. It is a life of surrender, of self-denial, of trust, of love and obedience. It is a life in which the living Christ functions as Lifegiver and Master, ordaining desire after His own spirit of love, sacrifice, and service. It is on this high plane of union and communion with Christ that the promise applies, "Ask whatsoever ye will, and it shall be done unto you." The "whatsoever" applies to desires to which Jesus subscribes, to desires in harmony with the will of God, to desires which express the consecration of a ransomed soul. Whatsoever we ask when Jesus is King of our desires shall be granted.

Is not this to contract the promise and make it practically no promise? By no means. Can anything better be conceived than that these hearts of ours should be filled with the indwelling Christ and that we should live and move and have our being in the truth which Jesus revealed? That we should know and love and do the will of God? That as far as our inner life is concerned, "we should always have all sufficiency for all things," finding that like Paul we "can do all things through Christ who gives us strength?" The promise of Jesus has in view true self-realization and self-expression which are possible only when the inner personal life draws constantly on Christ.

Every person may be justly regarded as a bundle of desires and the embodiment of a multitude of longings. It is not the promise of Jesus that, if we ask, these desires and longings shall be gratified without regard to the interests of personal character and God's use of us. But it is the promise of Jesus that we shall have what we ask if our desires conform to what God yearns to do for us and in us and through us. That is a wonderful promise which makes divine resources available for Christ-like character and service. In such a promise God speaks to our deepest needs and seeks to lure us to a way of life which will experience the true satisfaction of desire, and serve the ends of God's love for the world.

If we examine ourselves as to what we would like God to do for us and why we want Him to do it, we may be startled to find how fully our inner life is tuned to the note of utter selfishness. It is so easy to fail to do justice to the greatness of human nature, the possibilities of personality, and the good-will of God toward men. We crave power in one direction or another in order that we may wall ourselves in from our fellows and find repose and security in isolated self-sufficiency. The desire to abide in Christ and to have the whole inner nature saturated with His truth is not the dominant passion of our prayers. The apostle James strikes home when he says, "Ye ask, and receive not, because ye ask amiss, that ye may spend it in your pleasures."

They who abide in Christ and give free course to the truth of Christ in their own souls become possessed of desires far different from those which come to expression in a soul not thus anchored. They desire that Christ shall have the preeminence in all things. The joy of communion with Him sickens the soul of selfishness. The things that matter most are kept in the foreground: such things as keeping in the love of God and doing His will, such things as obedience to Christ and the reproduction of His life and spirit; such things as spiritual peace, enduring faith, transforming hope, and love like that of Jesus; such things as the testimony of a good conscience and the joy of work for Christ well done; such things as the sense of the high calling of God in Christ Jesus and the will of God that none should perish. In this vast field of fellowship with the Redeemer and likeness to Him the promised power functions and prayer is found to be an inspired weapon of safety and achievement.

If only we can come to desire the right things and to covet earnestly the best gifts, the glad discovery will follow that God is always and immediately available as the Giver of every good and perfect gift. Imagine a son of a well-to-do business man whose only interest in his father is in the money he can get from him! He has no desire to be a partner in his father's business, no longing to have fellowship with him, no appreciation of his father's love, no satisfaction in his company. He lives in a world of his own where the gratification of the mania for pleasure is the guiding star. He has recourse to his father only when it is to his personal interest to do so. The ideals of father and son are poles apart. The father craves to develop in the son the qualities of true manhood. He would fain have his son in business with him. If only the son could see it, nothing would please the father better than to be able to let his son share in all that he possesses. If only there were partnership in character, in ideals, in motive and service, partnership in everything else would readily follow. The son could have whatsoever he might desire if he showed himself to be in tune with his father's character and interests. But the son cannot see it and the father is forced in the interest of his son's well-being to restrain generosity, to impose limitations, and to withhold what he would so gladly place in the son's hands. Not otherwise is it in the relations between God and His children. The bestowal of power awaits moral fitness. The gifts of God are ready to drop into worthy hands. God looks for love and fellowship and consecration while we, alas too often, seek Him for the lesser gifts of material bounty. The qualifications in Jesus' promise are morally inevitable and ethically justified. They recall attention to the principles which control the bounty of God, principles which have reference to the true goal of our being and the work which God seeks to accomplish through us. These qualifications magnify the wisdom and grace of God and reveal the divine interest in holiness. They safeguard the interests of our souls and of the kingdom of God. They open up vast possibilities of commanding power but limit the realization to those who can be trusted with it. This is as it should be. If a man can reach a place where he can ask whatsoever he will and it shall be done unto him, it is important that such a man should be a man after God's own heart, that he should love men even as Christ loved them, that every desire should be the expression of good-will, that he should have a life and live a life drawn from the redeeming Prince of life, and that all the wonderful truth Jesus revealed should dominate that man's whole inner nature.

Power in prayer would be a curse if God entrusted it to men without discrimination. Recall the hymns of hate composed in one nation against another. In their hatred men utter imprecations, praying agonizing prayers that God will wreak vengeance on the objects of their wrath. If God responded to such diabolical passion and vehemence, this would be a sorry world.

There are those who hate law and order, who despise government, who covet riches and carnal pleasure; persons harboring demons of lust, avarice, and greed. If God promised to give such whatsoever they might ask, the full powers of hell would be let loose. Life would not be worth living. No moral interests could be conserved.

Avenues of power beckon. "Power belongeth unto God" and God is glad to share it with those who see eye to eye with Him. Get God's view of things, take His Word for things, do as He says, and you find yourself in possession of growing power, more and more able to be and to do all that carries out God's redeeming purpose for self and others. When Christ gets His way all things are ours. He gives free access to inexhaustible resources.

The Church Under Fire

PRAYER-HYMN

O Master of the changing road,
Direct me on the unknown way;
Make my poor heart Thy blest abode,
And suffer not my feet to stray.

O Master of unchanging love,
Thou mighty Friend through years of grace,
As to her window flies the dove,
So may my heart Thy will embrace.

O Master of the inner light,
Uphold me when the way is dark;
When Thy wise plan eludes my sight,
May I in faith press toward the mark.

O Master of my destiny,
Keep clear before my vagrant eyes,
The joy and power of life in Thee,
Be Thou the Way and Thou the Prize.

O Master of eternal life,
Lead on to Thine own victory,
To where awaits, beyond the strife,
The crown of immortality.

7

THE CHURCH UNDER FIRE

A man can no more be a Christian without facing evil and conquering it, than he can be a soldier without going to battle, facing the cannon's mouth, and encountering the enemy in the field. —E. H. CHAPIN

IT WAS FOR NO GOOD PURPOSE that the high priest asked Jesus about His disciples. Jesus was under arrest and the high priest was looking for some way of securing His condemnation. Unable to trap Jesus Himself, the high priest extended his inquiry to the disciples of Jesus in the hope that something might be brought to light which would justify the high priest in passing sentence on Jesus.

"The high priest therefore asked Jesus of his disciples." He could not ask the disciples themselves because they were not on hand to defend their Master. When Jesus was arrested the disciples forsook Him and fled. It was a mean thing to do. As they were leading Jesus away Peter followed afar off. John also followed, but they were not near enough to Jesus to be of service at the trial. It was a strange thing that the men who had been so intimate with Jesus should thus fail Him when He endured the contradiction of sinners.

The absence of the disciples impressed the high priest. It did not say much for Jesus that those who had been closest to Him should be absent when His life was at stake. A leadership that produces cowards is open to suspicion. Faithless Christians discredit Christ in the eyes of men like this high priest.

"The high priest therefore asked Jesus of his disciples." High priest though he was, he was an enemy of Jesus and a foe of true religion. Anyone making the claims that Jesus did is soon in peril when those who have acknowledged the claims turn traitor in a moment. The high priest was seeking not for truth, but for charges, and the most likely place to find them seemed to him to be the character of Jesus' followers.

The events of that memorable night are now a closed story. On the morrow Jesus was condemned and crucified. He trod the winepress alone. He drank the cup which His Father gave Him. But a sad feature of the record is the defection of His disciples and their failure to stand by in those last awful hours. And it is to be noted how much the high priest made of it, how he saw reason to dispose of Jesus because His followers showed a yellow streak.

Christ is still on trial. And He will always be on trial as long as the present world-order obtains. As His claims are pressed upon men they will seek to dispose of them by exposing His followers. They will be blind to the sinlessness of Jesus and all eyes to the sins and shortcomings of His disciples. The drab life of the Christian will obscure the wonderful life of the Christian's Master. The impotence of the disciples will hide the power of the Lord.

The world sees Christ as Christians reproduce Him or sees Him not because Christians fail to reflect Him. It is because there are so many feeble saints that there are so many unbelievers who never catch sight of the strong Son of God. Christ is crucified afresh every day because the Christ men see in the lives of Christians is not the true Christ.

The world sees the hypocrisy, the inconsistency, the selfishness, the lovelessness of the disciples and turns away in disgust. The world sees the divisions, the quarrels, the narrowness, and the antagonism of the followers of Jesus and forthwith erects a cross for Christ. It is not fair. But it is done. Christ is judged by His faithless friends and given a new cross because His followers prove traitors.

Christ took that risk when He committed His cause to His followers. He took that risk when He so trusted His disciples. He took that risk knowingly. He meant to take it. Such was His confidence in Himself that He was willing to commit the destiny of His cause to those who had seen and believed. He was willing to trust those who knew Him and professed to accept Him and love Him. He committed His honor to the care of His followers, confident that they would uphold it and spread it until every knee should bow and every tongue confess. What a motive to fidelity is this wonderful faith of Jesus in His disciples!

"The high priest therefore asked Jesus of his disciples." They were not there to testify to His wonderful teaching, His marvelous deeds, and His divine character. They were not present to tell what Jesus had meant to them and what irresistible convictions His life had quickened. Jesus was in the hands of His enemies and not a friend came forward to speak a good word for Him. And the high priest saw how Jesus was thus placed in a disadvantageous position and he made the most of it. What can Jesus say when those whom He trusted disappear in a crucial hour?

Jesus was abundantly able to take care of Himself. But the point is that His disciples failed Him at His trial and thus exposed Him to suspicion and condemnation. False witnesses gave perverted accounts of statements they had heard Jesus make and there were no disciples to give a true testimony. And Jesus' enemies pressed that fact of evident defection as an argument against Him. It looked bad. It lent itself to wrong interpretation. The enemies of Jesus were alert to seize any unfair advantage and His friends were without excuse in thus deserting their Master. They failed to show their faith by their works.

It is not difficult to expose the enemies of Christ who dispose of His claims by condemning His followers. They are not sincere. They are not lovers of truth and righteousness. They are not honest and fair. Their judgments are warped. Their attitude is prejudiced and biased. They will perish in their sins unless they repent and accept Christ. They have no right to reject Christ because Christians belie their name and drag the honor of their Lord into the mire. Do we dispute the value of a diamond when we note how many cheap imitations are worn by those who lack the real thing? Do we disparage law or medicine because the unworthy degrade the high standards of these professions? A true judgment overlooks the hypocritical and grounds itself on reality. As long as the character of Christ Himself stands unimpeached men will be without excuse in disposing of His claims to faith and obedience.

"The high priest therefore asked Jesus of his disciples." And the disciples are not without guilt if the inquiry gives cause for impugning of the Master. As a Christian takes his place in the world, the enemies of Christ should be made aware of the striking contrast in the spirit and behavior of His life. If the lust for pleasure is as strong in him as in them, the sufficiency of Christ is discredited. If his thirst for gold is as dominant as it is in those who do not follow Christ, it exposes the Master to slander. If a Christian is to all appearances no different from a worldling, where does Christ get any honor from his profession?

It is interesting to speculate as to what would have happened on the night of the betrayal if the disciples had not fled. If Peter had not followed afar off and had later been more concerned about standing by Jesus than about standing by the fire and warming himself, what splendid heroism on his part might now illumine the story of those tragic hours. We cannot help looking upon Peter standing by the fire and warming himself as typical. And the fire of coals is likewise easily made a symbol of the sources of satisfaction which the world makes to meet the needs of the soul. If Peter is thus seen standing by the fire warming himself and more concerned to get his share of the warmth than to defend his Master, even so great numbers of Christians are more concerned to get their share of creaturely goods and comforts than to promote the cause of Christ. It is this absence of contrast between the followers of Jesus and those who are not Christians which is so fatal to the growth of the body of believers.

The world builds many fires to combat the cold of a life without Christ. It builds the fires of wealth, of pleasure, of learning, of power, of fame, of social eminence, of new thought, of cults and isms and heresies without number. And it gathers around these fires because life is cold without the Saviour. Imagine their surprise when Christians gather around these fires also and show an eagerness to get warm not outdone by the most confirmed unbeliever. The surprise is ever expressing itself in queries which reveal that the worldling feels that there is something contradictory in this strange conduct of Christians. It is a veiled tribute to Christ that unbelievers should thus be impressed with the presence of disciples around the world's fires. Perhaps they have not been at ease in refusing Christ. Perhaps they are still cold in spite of all the world's fires. But here is Peter, one of the Master's disciples, pushing his way nearer to the fire. A fine Christian, says the worldling, to be so like the rest of us. And a fine Christ this Christ of Peter must be to be unable to wean His disciples away from our fires. With such followers, says the worldling, I want none of that leadership.

However illogical and unreasonable the position of those who reject Christ because of the worldliness of Christians, no one can deny that there are many that take this position, and the want of conformity to Christ in the lives of disciples is charged up to the Master Himself. The indifference of believers, their spiritual insensitiveness and irresponsibility, their inconsistencies and selfishness, their conformity to those who are without God and without hope in the world constitute barriers between possible disciples and Christ and prove in actual life to be harmful to His cause and derogatory to His claims.

There are many books that set forth the New Testament doctrine of the person and work of Christ. They are wonderful books, full of learning and insight, written with impelling conviction and power, setting before the reader a portrait of Christ calculated to inspire faith and worship. But the readers of these books are comparatively few and for the most part believers who bring a believing mind to the perusal. If we could get the unconvinced and the uncommitted to read these books with a sincere passion for truth, surely conviction would come to their souls. They would bow their heads in reverence and cry, "My Lord and my God." But the unsaved do not read these books. Cold as life is without Christ they are busy building fires at which to warm their hearts. The only apparent way in which these souls can be won for Christ is through the contagion of Christlike persons. They do not read books about Christ. They read only the actual lives of Christians with whom they come into contact. If these lives present no contrast to their own no saving influence is exerted. If the disciples are in nowise different from themselves they become confirmed in unbelief by the similarity. For them Christ is what His followers show Him to be. It is because Christ makes no visible difference to the way many of His disciples live that the uncommitted, the neutral, and the hostile persist in rejecting Him.

On the night of Jesus' arrest Peter was to all appearances just like everyone else who stood around the fire of coals. Yet what a difference, if only Peter had shown it! That very night he had been present when Jesus instituted the

Sacrament of the Lord's Supper. He had partaken of the bread and wine. He had heard the words of the great discourse. Yes, Peter had been with Jesus all through our Lord's ministry. He had seen His glory in the Mount. And here he is, denying his Master on the night in which Jesus was betrayed. How could he do it? How could he stand by that fire and warm himself like all the rest? How could he disclaim any knowledge of Jesus when, months before, he had shown enough knowledge to confess, "Thou art the Christ, the Son of the living God"? How could he prove so faithless?

Let the Christian who is without fault throw the first stone. As we mingle with men in the life of the world there are those who are hurrying Christ on to new condemnation. And too often have we been silent. The world has built its fires and we have joined the crowd and jostled others for a bit of warmth. Surely, we shall lay it to heart that Christ is still on trial and we shall pray for courage that our faith fail not. Even so, O Christ, may we be found true witnesses. For now it has come to this that the world is asking and sorely needing to be told about Christ by those who know Him. We are proclaiming Christ as the world's only hope, and whether men have heard the proclamation or not, they find no adequate goal for life apart from him. Events transpire which call for resources of which they are not possessed: events where material wealth does not count and knowledge is mere ignorance; events which baffle, crush, and deplete life; events that test the souls and expose its poverty. Under these circumstances Christ's true followers are to lift Him up in His glory as Saviour and Lord, to tell the difference He has made in them and can make in all. The cause of Christ is with His followers, and to bring needy souls into contact with the Redeemer is their high call. When life is bankrupt for want of Christ or is bankrupt while deluded with false claims of solvency, it must be told what Christ is competent to be and do in men. "Jesus Christ, coming from the open heart of the Godhead, reveals the love that burns there; and men who catch the flame from Him, kindle its fire all through the world."

Not high priests now, but needy souls everywhere, working for that which is not bread, perish for want of light and leading and testimony which only those who are truly in Christ are qualified to offer and that in terms of personal experience at the hands of the great Physician of souls. Let those who without Christ shiver around the world's fires behold in Christians life of genial warmth and sustained enthusiasm far from these fires which yield no satisfying warmth and they will begin seeking the hidden fire of God's redeeming grace in Christ which does satisfy those called by Christ's name. "If the light and fire of heaven burn in one heart, every other heart within its range is touched by the glow; the radiance of the indwelling Godhead by its mere presence radiates from the life that holds it." Faithful witness will lure to the Saviour. "The story must be told."

The church is too much under fire for want of the true fire of God's purifying and invigorating Spirit. Love for the world's fires and for the human resources of well-being quenches the fire of the Holy Spirit. A church on fire for God and souls will be fired with the testimony of spiritual reality and the witness thus borne will commend the Saviour and prevent His repeated crucifixion. "Let the redeemed of the Lord say so." They are the proof of what Christ can do. Christ rests His plea on their witness. He is enthroned or crucified according to their testimony.

The Old-Fashioned Mother

MOTHER

She lives in quiet faithfulness,
And covets not the world's renown,
Content, if God her labor bless,
To bring her own to worthy crown.

Her gentle deeds of mothering,
Instinct with love that understands,
Bring to each child in everything
The comfort of her heart and hands.

If schooled by want to do without,
She makes a pittance stretch to more,
And by her thrift puts fear to rout,
Achieving much with little store.

In tender acts of sacrifice,
She wields a queenly power for good,
And bears in love at any price
The burdens of her motherhood.

Nor tasks nor tests embarass her,
She meets them in a mother's way,
The quiet strength of character
Enables her to win the day.

8

THE OLD-FASHIONED MOTHER

When Eve was brought to Adam . . . he did not style her wife, but simply mother, — mother of all living creatures. In this consists the glory and the most precious ornament of woman. —LUTHER

THE OLD-FASHIONED MOTHER is often pictured in life's eventide. She is sitting in a rocking chair. The Bible is in her lap. Perhaps she is looking over her spectacles. Her hair is turned to silver. Her figure is in repose.

Think today of the old-fashioned mother in the full strength of years. Her way of dressing may seem quaint to modern eyes. But what a woman she was! She was first out of bed. She always got up on time. She had no need of an alarm clock. It was mother who called father when breakfast was well under way. It was mother who called the children and got them ready for school or work.

She prepared meals, washed dishes, scrubbed pots and pans and cleaned the house from cellar to attic. Sewing and mending were part of the daily round. She made her own clothes. She made clothes for the children. She could take an old overcoat of father and make a new suit out of it for one of her boys.

She lived before there were vacuum sweepers, electric washers, electric sewing machines, frigidaires, electric irons, electric toasters, electric fans, and such like. House work was one hundred percent hand-work. Brain and muscle went into the daily task. We marvel today and wonder how she stood it.

She reared a large family. When a new baby came a kinswoman or neighbor would lend a friendly hand for a spell. Two weeks later she was about her work as usual and a voice from the cradle told of added cares and joys.

The old-fashioned mother looked upon father as the head of the house. Children were impressed with his authority. They were taught to respect him. Mother referred to him as the court of last appeal. Thus there was unity in home and family life. Mother pulled for father. Father and mother pulled together. Children were children. Father was the head of the home. Mother was the power behind the throne.

The Bible draws her picture with a rew deft strokes. "She worketh willingly with her hands. She riseth also while it is yet night, and giveth meat to her household. She girdeth her loins with strength, and strengtheneth her arms. Her candle goeth not out by night. Strength and honor are her clothing. She openeth her mouth with wisdom, and in her tongue is the law of kindness. She looketh well to the ways of her household, and eateth not the bread of idleness."

There was a family altar in the old-fashioned home. Father was priest to his own family and mother was the priestess of the domestic hearth. She kept the children attentive while father read from the Bible. Mother saw to it that the children kept their eyes shut while father prayed. It is hard for children to keep their eyes shut. It was equally hard for mother to keep her eyes partly open in order to see to it that the children kept theirs shut. Who can forget this tender watchfulness of mother while father lifted mother and children in prayer to the everlasting arms? The whole scene, repeated day after day in sincerity and reverence, promoted the cause of true religion. Children were taught to count God in and put God first.

The old-fashioned mother managed somehow to have her quiet hour. Room was made for the nurture of mind and spirit. Devotional reading of the Bible was a habit with her. She would not think of doing without her church paper. She kept up with the Sunday-school lessons and the children's catechism. She often sang at her work and the substance of her singing included the great hymns of the church. No one could come in touch with mother without finding out that Christ was the unseen Guest in heart and home.

The old-fashioned Christian mother loved the church. She was glad when the hour of worship came. She was eager not only to attend church but to work for the church. She was active in the Ladies' Aid Society and in the Woman's Missionary Society. Many a quilting party witnessed her zeal for the Lord. If unable to attend a service or a meeting she saw to it that her gift was there. It was with fervor that she used to sing,

> I love Thy Church, O God!
> Her walls before Thee stand,
> Dear as the apple of Thine eye
> And graven on Thy hand.
>
> For her my tears shall fall,
> For her my prayers ascend;
> To her my cares and toils be given
> Till cares and toils shall end.
>
> Beyond my highest joy
> I prize her heavenly ways,
> Her sweet communion, solemn vows,
> Her hymns of love and praise.

It is pleasing to recall how the old-fashioned Christian mother's hopes for her children were linked with prayer that God might help them to love and trust the Saviour. Deep down in her heart was a longing that God might honor a son or daughter with a call to dedicate life to Christian service. As women in Israel hoped for the honor of becoming the mother of the Messiah, so the mothers we honor today prayed for the distinction of having a son enter the Gospel ministry or becoming a missionary to lands afar. Many a Christian mother has had the holy joy of giving a son or daughter to a life of Christian leadership. We recall today how much this was in their thought, how deeply they prized the honor of furnishing workers for God's vineyard, and how sweet was sacrifice when it meant a child for the pulpit or the mission field.

The old-fashioned Christian mother valued character more than money and regarded the making of a living as subordinate to the making of a life. Her influence was on the side of the good, the true, the morally beautiful. She insisted on the priceless worth of "clean hands and a pure heart." Nothing was desirable to her that meant the sacrifice of honor and integrity. She coveted for her children the best gifts. She was interested in attainments without taint. Happy the man whose mother was a conscience to him! The memory of such a mother is one of the controlling forces of life. "She being dead yet speaketh."

The old-fashioned Christian mother took seriously the vows made at the baptism of her children. She made work of it to instruct her children in "the truths of God's Word and in the way of salvation through Jesus Christ." She prayed for her children and taught them to pray. She trained them "in all holy living." Her supreme desire was that her children might "enjoy eternal life both in this world and in the world to come." One of the happiest days of her life was the Lord's Day when one of her children was publicly received into the fellowship of the church. If there was a black sheep or a stray lamb, how the old-fashioned Christian mother shepherded that soul! What ingenuity of love! What resourcefulness in prayer! What patience and persistence of endeavor! Faithfully she took her cross and followed Christ in winning the wayward. She never gave up. On all the Calvaries of the world where sin slays its tens of thousands you will find mothers receiving the sword into their bosoms, loving till death and loyal to the end.

The old-fashioned mother looked upon children as a heritage of the Lord. A childless marriage was never the result of purpose. If death removed a mother and left a number of children without a mother's care there were mothers who took them in. There was always room for one more.

The old-fashioned mother is not extinct. She is still with us, living the simple life, finding her career in a home, in rearing the children, and being a true help-meet to her husband. Mother love is one of the abiding forces of human society. It is still a wholesome, healing power. It still tends to purify and sweeten. It is God's bread to hungry hearts. It is water of life to all.

Deep down in the heart of them mothers ring true. No honor given them is too much. The very name "mother" means that they have been in the valley of the shadow of death. No one can measure their love. By unwearied service and sacrifice they care for their children and seek their good. A mother's love helps mankind to believe in the love of God.

Men credit the mothers of the race with every conceivable virtue. Hers is the purity of the lily, the fragrance of the rose, the beauty of the orchid, the grace of all moral loveliness. Her heart is a holy shrine, her mind a treasury of all that is good, her imaginaton a creator of paradise, her disposition incarnate kindness, and her ways the ways of pleasantness and peace.

Every man gratefully acknowledges the refining, ennobling, strengthening influence of the mother of his children. Her comradeship in the battles of life has meant the difference between victory and defeat. "The heart of her husband doth safely trust in her." "Her children arise up, and call her blessed; her husband also, and he praiseth her."

Christ and Christian Destiny

FACE LIFE WITH CHRIST

Trust in Jesus, build on Christ,
Nothing human has sufficed;
Self a victim? Christ is Lord,
Faith in Christ will peace afford.

Tempted, tried, afflicted, down?
Vain seems hope of victor's crown?
Life with Jesus in control
Means salvation for the soul.

Sickness, weakness, suffering,
Seem to threaten everything?
Threats as threats are false alarms,
Christ the fears and foes disarms.

Sea of life, rough, tempest-tossed?
Nothing vital can be lost.
Ne'er a storm God's will retards,
Christ makes billows boulevards.

Harken, souls, in grief and pain!
Find it hard to see the gain?
Christ employs refiner's fire,
Perfecting divine desire.

Leave it all to Christ the King,
Christ is bound to make us sing;
Golden harvests, ripe through tears,
Will be ours when Christ appears.

Faith in Jesus cannot lose,
Self or Christ, one has to choose;
Self-reliance cannot win,
Christ the Door can put you in.

9

CHRIST AND CHRISTIAN DESTINY

Death is as the foreshadowing of life. We die that we may die no more. —HERMAN HOOKER

AN OPTIMISTIC AUTHOR has given to one of his books the title *Daybreak Everywhere* which is suggestive of what the resurrection of Jesus means to Christians. The resurrection has brought daybreak everywhere. The light of the resurrection morning streams on all the ways of human experience, shedding divine radiance on every dark and cloudy day, and dispelling even the grim shadows of the valley of death. The night is far spent for those who have eyes to see the glory of the first Easter dawn. Christ risen means the triumphant return of our Lord from "the last weariness, the final strife." Unbaffled now by lingering mysteries, we labor on in hope, confidently expecting a vindication of faith proportionate to the splendid reality of our Saviour's victory. Already it is daybreak everywhere, and the signs of dawn repose caressingly on every event and problem previously wrapped in inscrutable night.

For once the eternal fitness of things was duly served and marvelously expressed in the resurrection of Jesus from the dead. For once! Enough surely continues rampant which shocks our sense of the fitness of things, violating the proprieties of a moral order, challenging, defying and denying faith, with right on the scaffold and wrong on the throne, situations where vice flourishes and virtue languishes and where the actual holds the ideal up to contempt. But the resurrection of Jesus is the standard proof of the integrity of the universe and we feel that here is a case where ideal and actual unite in righteous identity.

That young atheist of whom we have read expressed it. He determined to examine the Christian religion. He began by studying the Gospel of John. He came to the wise conclusion, "That Jesus who is portrayed in the Gospel of John is either the Saviour of the world or he ought to be." Such is the verdict of right-thinking people with reference to the resurrection of Jesus. If it were the case that no resurrection were recorded of Jesus, if the death that He died closed the account of His life, we should instinctively feel, "This Jesus who is portrayed in the Gospels either rose from the dead or he ought to have risen from the dead."

This sense of "oughtness," of moral propriety and eternal fitness, with reference to the resurrection of Christ, attests the daybreak which has dawned upon the human spirit through the fact which Easter commemorates. Without the Easter fact hope deferred would long since have made the heart sick unto death in a world where current actualities are constantly blighting expectation that things will ever be as they ought to be. If Christ be not risen, there might have persisted for a time a grim and mournful acquiescence to things as they were, but it is incredible that civilization could have survived till now such a colossal prostitution of justice as the doing to death of the best man that ever lived. "But now is Christ risen from the dead" and become accountable for a spiritual resurrection in unnumbered millions creative of that vast realm of faith and insight in the heart of man which makes possible and pertinent any idea of the eternal fitness of things.

Imagine the depression of the disciples and friends of Jesus and of all lovers of righteousness when the body of Jesus was laid in the tomb. Such an issue of such a life was enough to sink His cause beyond rescue and to paralyze moral idealism for all time. The mystery of iniquity would envelop mankind in eternal night if the spirit that would kill God were shown to be the prevailing power. The only possible conclusion of such infamous triumph would be that "the pillared firmament is rottenness and earth's base stubble."

It is easily apparent how representative Jesus was in what He suffered, how really He was in our stead, how, like David facing Goliath alone for his country, Jesus was facing the power of sin for all mankind in His own person. The complete story of what happened to Him would become standard for the interpretation of every individual life. If death be final for one such as He, there is nothing to be said by way of hope for any man. He is the test-case, revealing whether there is a God who can be trusted, whether or not there is a moral order or any eternal fitness of things to be expressed and served, speaking the authoritative word on the destiny of man, bringing to light whether or not righteousness and love have any chance of life and victory in a world where sin reigns in death.

Thus the battle was on and matters between God in His love and man in his sin were brought to a head. The seeming triumph of wrong was only for the purpose of allowing the venom of sin to exhaust its powers and demonstrate its futility. When the last bit of poison had worked itself in and out in the bosom of our sinless and imperishable representative, He came forth from the tomb to herald a new morning for the world and to suffuse daybreak everywhere. And thus it is that there has prevailed in the world this sense of the eternal fitness of things. The resurrection of Jesus has vindicated faith not only in Him, but faith in the rightness of right and its final triumph, faith in the preeminence of love over hate, faith in the goodness of God and His purpose and power to bring goodness to ultimate victory, faith that "life is ever lord of death" and that "love can never lose its own."

We still see and suffer from the prevalence of crime and lawlessness and hate and greed and vice and strife, and chief among these factors in the misery of mankind is the sable figure of Death, who steals away our loved ones and draws ever nearer to gather us also into his lordly and dreaded embrace. But the empty tomb and the glory of the risen Saviour restore our confidence and quicken the assurance that the fruits of His victory are even now in the hand of faith. We shall weather every gale and reach home at last.

> In heavenly love abiding,
>   No change my heart shall fear;
> And safe is such confidinug,
>   For nothing changes here;
> The storm may roar without me,
>   My heart may low be laid,
> But God is round about me,
>   And can I be dismayed?
> In heavenly love abiding,

The resurrection of Jesus has a bearing on our view of God and the world, on our appraisal of life, and our part in it and reaction to it. Therefore we must not fail to count it in, to let its light and influence play on our minds. In a case at court judge and jury want all the facts. They require every available bit of evidence. How otherwise can the verdict be true? We are prone to pass judgment on life. The question is, "Have we before us all the facts?" If so, the fact that Christ is risen from the dead is among them and it changes the bearing of all the other facts.

To illustrate: Jesus taught what is called the doctrine of God's Providence. In practical language this is the truth of God's Fatherly love and care. Remember how Jesus in the Sermon on the Mount urged His hearers not to take anxious thought for the morrow. He laid it upon their hearts that our heavenly Father knows our needs and is a generous Provider. The apostle Paul frames the matter into a definite proposition when he says, "We know that all things work together for good to them that love God." Now in view of many facts of general human experience this teaching of Jesus and this statement of Paul are truly amazing. There are many things taking place all the time which seem to give the lie to God's sovereign love and Fatherly care. Terrible things happen which can only be described as due to "an act of God." They seem utterly gratuitous, serve no useful purpose that anyone can see, and if wrought by man would be condemned as expressions of pure malice. People are heard to say that if there be a God, He is either lacking in love or in power. They cannot see how God can fail to interfere in the way things are going if He has the character of a Father and power to make the world as it ought to be. The reasoning is not at all profound. A ready answer might be given. Allusion is made to it for the purpose of pointing out that we hear many insisting that life is only a game of chance.

If life is only a game of chance, the only chance the bulk of mankind has is to lose. Opposed to that theory is the teaching of Scripture that life is in the heavenly Father's care and keeping, under the control of sovereign love, with the guarantee that no one will finally lose out who trustfully places his life in God's mighty hand. Which is the true view? The standard fact in the matter is what happened to Jesus. When you see Him on the Cross crying, "My God, my God, why hast Thou forsaken me" it would seem to establish that God did not care. And when presently He gave up the ghost the stunned disciples might have declared that there was no God to care either for Jesus or themselves. They might have gone on to say that there is no God of sovereign love who cares for truth and righteousness and service and sacrifice. They might have moaned, "Life is only a game of chance." But not for long. The dawn of a new day was speeding on. They received the startling message of the empty tomb. They saw the risen Lord. It was daybreak everywhere. They waited for the promised power and got it. They went forth to change the currents of the world's thought and life. The cross of Jesus was seen to be in the light of His resurrection the highest proof of God's Fatherly love and care, both for themselves and the world. It was seen to be for Jesus the stepping-stone to a new throne of glory. There was no doubt for them now about God's love and power and purpose, no doubt at all about the supremacy of truth and righteousness and sacrifice and life. All virtues shone with regal splendor. Life stood forth in the radiance of spiritual meaning. Sin and wrong and death were temporary and ultimately doomed and futile. Gaze where they would, above, beneath, around, into the past or into the future, it was daybreak everywhere.

The resurrection of Jesus changed everything that was dark and sinister and mysterious. Can anyone imagine the disciples on the resurrection morning saying that life is only a game of chance? Had anyone reminded them of their despair at the death of Jesus they would have said, "We spoke too hastily. We spoke before we had all the facts. God forgive us for doubting Him."

God did far more for the world and its moral interests and spiritual destiny by giving Jesus over to the bitter and shameful death of the cross and then raising Him from the dead than He would have done by saving Him from the cross. It is the standard instance of the ages of God's sovereignty in love and wisdom and power, and shows beyond the shadow of a doubt the reality and integrity of the assurance that "all things work together for good to them that love God."

We incline to judge God and appraise life before we have all the facts. We overlook the fact of the risen Lord and its bearing on our personal problems. We are loathe to wait until God gets through with us. We hesitate to trust

Him and to give Him a free hand. We forget the need of the refiner's fire. We crave fair weather and a smooth sea, forgetful that "a smooth sea never made a skillful mariner." Many can see love only in luxury, unmindful of the leanness of soul found in the lap of fortune. The way of the cross preceded the glory of the resurrection. The fact of a risen Lord brings to us the assurance that when in God's Providence we come to our Gethsemane and some impending cross bids us "lay in dust life's glory dead," our heavenly Father has in view some wondrous crown which will symbolize for us forever the divine purpose of grace in our lives.

Creatures of sense as we are, we are not readily amenable to visions of an eternal future, but in the risen Christ God lures us with the first-fruits of His coming harvest. The sight of the soul is directed to God's plan for our ultimate destiny. Our persistence as complete persons, including a body, is guaranteed. What we are to be and whither we are going is certified to us in the risen Saviour. We are moving on to victory and to reunion in eternity. The best is yet to be. The triumph of Christ is grandly social. It is an achievement which is prophetic. Given only faith in Christ and God would make it the earnest of every man's destiny. Unbelief is the only barrier to appropriation and realization. It is daybreak everywhere. "But now hath Christ been raised from the dead, the firstfruits of them that are asleep" (1 Corinthians 15:20). For people who sit in darkness, the light has shined, enough light to lead home to God.

What Shall I Do with Jesus?

CONSCIENCE SPEAKING

I must be true to Jesus,
    He gave His life for me;
He left His home in glory,
    And died upon a tree.
His life was full self-giving
    In deeds of wondrous grace;
In loving, sinless living
    He, only, kept the pace.

He makes His home within me,
    Bestows all daily needs;
He handles all my problems,
    My constant prayers He heeds.
He knows my every weakness,
    Forsees each fiery test,
Provides the undergirding
    To keep me at my best.

Supreme among my treasures,
    A wealth untold is He;
The river of His pleasures
    Makes life a feast to me.
The riches of His mercy,
    In everflowing tide,
For me, a poor weak sinner,
    New heart and hope provide.

I must be true to Jesus,
    The Son of God is He,
Who made a full atonement
    For sinners just like me.
He rose, to heaven ascended,
    At God's right hand to be;
And through the Holy Spirit
    He lives and reigns in me.

10

WHAT SHALL I DO WITH JESUS?

Ignorance never settles a question. —Disraeli

PILATE was under obligation to answer his own question. He alone was authorized in the circumstances to decide the issue before him. He was convinced that Jesus should receive a favorable judgment. "For he knew that for envy they had delivered him." If Pilate, with his assurance of Jesus' innocence, was not man enough to render a verdict of truth, how could the accusers of Jesus be expected to demand his release?

Pilate had all the light he needed and the necessary authority to do what was right. He surrendered to the mob a question which was his alone. Hence he came under the power of the mob and what they did to Jesus that day they first of all did to Pilate's soul. Pilate opened his soul to devils and they forthwith made it a stronghold of hell.

Pilate did what he did and so the case stands. But Jesus is still on trial and every one who knows Him is under necessity to decide the question, "What then shall I do with Jesus which is called Christ?"

Some questions do not much concern us. It does not matter to our character and destiny whether or not we render a judgment as to the authorship of the plays credited to Shakespeare, as to the relative might of pen or sword, as to the comparative destructiveness of fire or water and other similar questions. It is no disgrace or menace to our future to say that we have not gone into these matters sufficiently to render an intelligent decision.

Other questions are more personal and vital. Shall I be honest? Shall I keep my life pure? Shall I be kind? Such questions form a test of character and effect the interests of the soul. It is not a matter of indifference how these deeper questions are answered. They are moral questions and involve conscience. Decision one way or the other is productive of weal or woe and ranges life on the side of God or against Him.

So the question, "What shall I do then with Jesus which is called Christ?" is personal, vital, inevitable, unavoidable. It tests what we are, what we seek, what we worship, what we love. The question comes home to the heart and Jesus presses for a personal decision with reference to His redeeming love and Lordship. We are personally charged with the answer. The responsibility for decision cannot be surrendered to the unbelieving world. Their decision is made already. "Let him be crucified" is the verdict of blind prejudice. But every one who shares a truer persuasion must answer the question, "What shall I do then with Jesus which is called Christ."

The personal pronoun looms large in this question. Jesus already knows what the world will do with Him and what it is doing with Him every day. It is crucifying Him and will crucify Him until such time as He returns to destroy it with the breath of His mouth. Meanwhile, He draws near in love to press His claims, to offer the riches of His grace, to see what disposition we will make of Him who seeks crowning at our hands. We cannot get rid of Him, so strong is His desire to keep us from allying ourselves with the mob or with Pilate. And if we will look only at Him and lose sight of the crowd and listen only to Him and be deaf to the clamor of unbelief, we shall be stronger to face our responsibility and to decide, as we know we should, the tremendously personal question, "What shall I do with Jesus?"

There is only Jesus and I in the question. It is as if nobody else existed or had a say in the matter. Decision cannot be evaded. To put it off is to decide against Him. There is only Jesus and I and yet, not only these, for in that case how could we do aught but trust and love and obey Him? There is someone or something or many and much which comes between the two, claiming our trust and obedience to Him. Someone or something or perhaps many and much which can only be ours as we surrender Jesus to be crucified. Shining paths open alluringly before us leading to varied golden rewards of a life of self-will. Splendid prizes almost vocally cry, "Let him be crucified." Some earthly paradise comes within the vision with trees laden with forbidden but luscious fruit and we would fain partake thereof were it not for the inescapable question, "What shall I do then with Jesus?" It is Jesus crowned or Jesus crucified. The Christward reference of our choices is always there, fatefully, irresistibly there. Jesus will not be pushed aside. We are tested and challenged at every point and nothing is right until Christ has His crown at our hands.

Suppose we are tempted to ways of selfish desire and are about to make a bargain with our tempters. Suppose we are almost yielding to some way of life where Christ cannot go with us. Suppose we see the goal of ambition or passion in sight and to be presently reached if only we do not stand on principle. "What shall I do then with Jesus which is called Christ?" Shall we repay His love with hatred, His sacrifice with self-assertion, His faithfulness with treachery, His loyalty to our eternal interests with base denial?

Christ is always a partner in the moral alternatives which confront the soul. In every issue affecting character and destiny He is present, silently and appealingly, awaiting our verdict. And the price of having our own selfish will is always the crucifixion of Jesus. The voices which bid us consult expediency, profit, pleasure, distinction and position are voices which in effect bid us crucify Jesus. There is also the still, small voice of the Spirit with which God speaks, "This is my Son, hear ye him." Voices versus the Voice, the mob versus the Man, the cross versus the crown. Thus the amazing alternatives press upon the spirit and the soul, in conflict courting life or death. Thus every hour of moral crisis is big with destiny. It is with us to say whether Jesus shall go bearing His cross or stay wearing His crown, the cross or the crown of our fashioning.

The One, Only Saviour

CREED

Jesus, Saviour, Christ the Lord,
   Christ as Son of God adored,
Breathe in us this worthy end:
   Man my brother, God my Friend.

Grant us faith to conquer fear,
   Love to feel all creatures dear;
To Thy will may self-will bend,
   Man my brother, God my Friend.

By Thy Spirit, Prince of Peace,
   Rule the world that wars may cease,
Love and law in service blend,
   Man my brother, God my Friend.

Source and Guide of happy life,
   Lead us out of greed and strife,
Into ways that serve Thy end,
   Man my brother, God my Friend.

11

THE ONE, ONLY SAVIOUR

Who for us men and for our salvation came down from heaven. —The Nicene Creed

No one has ever been able to take from Jesus His peculiar glory of being the Saviour. After nineteen hundred years this statement still stands. Millions have rejoiced in His salvation and the millions who have not rejoiced in His salvation have no salvation in which to rejoice. The exclusive preeminence of leading men from spiritual death into spiritual life belongs to Jesus only. Here surely is the proof of what Peter claims for Jesus that the history of the world from that day to this has shown it to be even as he said.

No wonder that these who have experience of the competence of Jesus in the matter of their salvation are jealous of His glory. They have long been aware of their own incompetence and the incompetence of every pretender. Why should it be thought a matter of indifference that efforts to discredit Jesus in this His solitary uniqueness are current and clamorous? Even though He that sitteth in the heavens shall laugh and the Lord shall hold in derision those who impugn the Saviour, we cannot refrain from coming to the help of the Lord in this matter. Experienced deliverance shall find voice in praise of the Deliverer.

Sure that there is salvation in none other, but that there is salvation in Him, the story must be told. For this is how it was and this is what happened. "But now in Christ Jesus ye that were once far off have been brought nigh by the blood of Christ. *Far off!* This is how it was. *Brought nigh!* This is what happened. We were far out of the way and were brought into it and Jesus did it. And the redeemed of the Lord will declare, every man in his own tongue, what it means to be what he was and to be what he is. For there is diversity of gifts, albeit one Spirit. But the witness shall be heard both with Pentecostal vigor and Pentecostal variety.

No itemized account can do justice to the great salvation. But it includes darkness turned to light, ignorance dispelled by knowledge, bondage issuing in freedom, being dead transformed into being alive, fear and distrust giving place to confidence and peace, shackles broken, burdens lifted, guilt removed, pollution cleansed, and all things new. It was like being born again, beginning life anew and then such a life. It was like removing from the sphere of sin and death into a sphere of righteousness and life, leaving behind whatever oppressed us there and entering here into what is only and altogether energizing and sustaining. But the Mover was Jesus who took us in our impotence and placed us by His competence in the kingdom of His grace. The tattered garments of self-sufficiency and the filthy rags of self-righteousness, which so ill became us, were discarded and the one only Saviour put on us the robe of His own righteousness, that we might feel at home in the new life. And now there is perfect freedom and abundant life and unbroken fellowship with God and fullness of joy in the growing consciousness of a mighty redemption. And He to whom we owe it all makes us serviceable by the inspiration of His love. All this and much more those saved by the Saviour have reason to tell.

"Not unto us, not unto us, but unto his name be glory." For it was not in us to escape from the evil and attain the good. Nor in any other man or in anything else whatsoever. Only in the name of Jesus was our salvation accomplished. His was the power, to Him be the glory. Ours was the pardon, to Him be the praise.

What are the facts which establish the solitary significance of Jesus as the Saviour of men? First and foremost and fundamental is the fact that He died for our sins according to the Scriptures. This fact does not please the natural man who is incapable of appraising himself as God sees him. It is confidently affirmed that the way to God is always open irrespective of what Jesus did, but even this confidence reposes on what Jesus has revealed concerning the Fatherly love of God. The genuine Christian, however, is in accord with the fact in this matter, in believing in Jesus as the sin-bearer who took our place of condemnation and achieved our deliverance from God's holy wrath against sin. Were it not for our trust in Christ as a person of such dignity and importance both in relation to God and to man that the Lord could lay on Him the iniquity of us all, we could have no assurance of pardon and hence no peace.

With the millions of Christians it has always been even so. It has been only as full value has been given to the fact that Jesus has fully met the claims of God's righteousness, not only in our interest but in our place, that the trusting soul has experienced the joy of full assurance. Some have been so mournfully conscious of their sins that forgiveness by the blood of Christ has seemed too wonderful a boon for them to be able to believe that they were included in its benefits. Others of mature Christian experience have known days when their sins loomed like black clouds in their sky and peace would have been impossible if it had depended on aught else or less than the perfect sacrifice of the Son of God. Like Martin Luther they looked within, and looking within they could only cry, "My sin, my sin." But looking away from self to Christ crucified, they found peace in the sin-bearer.

This is the standard Christian experience. It is at every point in perfect harmony with moral reality. It is not a case of Jesus being more forgiving than God and overcoming

God's wrath by dying. Jesus is God, veiled in flesh. The Son and the Father are one. It is a case of God bearing man's sins in Christ and bearing them away by the suffering of death. What Jesus did, God did. What Jesus suffered, God suffered. This underlies our confidence in Jesus' competence to bear our sins. Trust in Jesus is trust in God. The forgiveness of sins is neither cheap nor easy. Only God can forgive because all sin is against God. And when God forgives it must not be in violence to His character. So God Himself assumes the burden of making forgiveness possible and actual and the means employed is the sacrifice of His Son. All things are possible with God, even the forgiveness of sins. Great is the mystery, but it is not for us to say how God shall do it. He has lifted His Son before the eyes of the world and bids us trust Christ crucified and this trust brings the pardon. In default of human sin-bearers, it needs but God, albeit all of God, and Jesus, who was the fullness of the Godhead bodily, is the one saving name. In none other is there salvation. No other is needed. He is the one perfect sacrifice for sins forever. "And in none other is there salvation: for neither is there any other name under heaven, that is given among men, whereby we must be saved" (Acts 4:12).

The blessedness of trust in Jesus is just this that it rids us of the burden of our sin; that it removes the guilt of it, cleanses the pollution of it and destroys the power of it; that it removes the barriers between the soul and God, thus allowing the tide of God's regenerating Spirit to come in! Sin is a thick cloud and forgiveness is its removal so that the trusting heart may find life and light in the sunshine of God's love. And if sin may be likened to a disease, a humanly incurable disease which puts the seal of death on the soul's true life, Jesus is the Physician who eradicates it from the system by the infusion of His redeeming blood. All that sin brings, Jesus casts out. All that sin causes the loss of, Jesus brings back. To be delivered from the death which sin spreads over our inner life and to gain a name and a place in the redeemed family of God, this is salvation and eternal life. To be saved in that sense is the unique, preeminent and divine work of Christ, which cost Him His life and gained Him His crown as the only name under heaven given among men whereby we must be saved.

Partners with God

PRAYER FOR REVIVAL

Pray on, Christian, pray, believing,
God is giving, man receiving;
Grace for grace is still the rule.
Hasten thus the Lord's arrival,
And a Holy Ghost revival;
What a joy to be God's tool!
Heated by God's holy fire,
You shall have your heart's desire:
For the body perfect healing,
For the soul ecstatic feeling,
For the work God's perfect power.
Halleluiah, what a power
When God's mercy strikes the hour!
Keep on praying, praying, praying!
God for reason is delaying.
O, for faith to claim the promise;
Not to be like doubting Thomas.
Lord, in mercy, pardon sin,
Lord, Thy promised reign bring in;
Millions, millions, crave the day,
Jesus, Saviour, come to stay.

12

PARTNERS WITH GOD

It is good for us to think that no grace or blessing is truly ours till we are aware that God has blessed some one else with it through us. —PHILLIPS BROOKS

HERE IS a big inspiring idea and ideal: A Christian a partner with God. God is in business in human society and every Christian is called to be a partner in the business. What is God's business?

God is in the business of undoing the mischief of sin, destroying its power and freeing life from slavery to it. God is in the business of recreating human personalities in Christ Jesus and making them children of God. A Christian is a partner with God in this business.

God is in the business of seeking and saving that which is lost. This divine Crusade of redemption heads up in Jesus Christ, the Son of God, who became man for our salvation, purchasing eternal life for us by the sacrifice of His own sinless life. This saving operation of God in Jesus Christ is the biggest business ever done in service of mankind. The story of that act of God must be told. The telling is big business and Christians the world over are partners in the business.

God is in the business of begetting a people for Himself. His saving acts to secure this end are written in a book, the Bible. God has lodged His divine power in that book, so that instruction in it is followed by the results God intends. "It pleased God by the foolishness of preaching to save them that believe." Teaching the truth of the Word of

God wherever or whenever is an effective form of preaching and the teacher and doer of it is a partner with God in it.

God is in the business of establishing His rule in the hearts of men. He deems it important to begin with the child. Mighty forces of the world beat upon the susceptible nature of the child. They assail the child by way of the newspaper, the magazine, the movies, the radio and all the influences of a secularized, mechanized, godless age. Through Christian parents, pastors and teachers, God means to bring to bear upon the mind and heart of the younger generation the full impact of His saving truth. It is big business to overcome the forces which blast with powers which redeem and bless. Fathers, mothers, pastors, and teachers are partners with God in that business.

God is in the business of building the Kingdom of God in this world, the Kingdom which is righteousness and peace and joy in the Holy Ghost. Vast miseries call loudly for social justice. Organized evils hold millions in bondage. The trail of the serpent besmirches the fairest handiwork of God. The earth is drenched with the blood of man's inhumanity to man. That blood cries to God and God answers the cry with the blood shed for our redemption. The Christian believer knows the only way out of the dark for the world. A new race is in the making in the homes and Bible schools of the land. A part of God's big business of bringing back a statelier Eden to men is the teaching of the children, indoctrinating them in God's saving truth. Whoever shares in Christian education is a partner with God in this business.

God is in the business of producing Christian character, creating moral atmosphere, environing human hearts with a climate of holiness, furnishing developing personalities with ideals and inspiration. All this is intended to be to the spirit of growing childhood what sunshine and wholesome food and proper activity and needed rest are to the physical life of a child. Here a teacher functions with light and love and leading. It is God's business, because it is a work for which only God is equal; but every one who works for God is in it.

God has erected a long battle-line against advancing forces of unrighteousness and at this and that point of the struggle between good and evil, frontal attacks are part of God's strategy. Rescue missions attempt to capture moral derelicts for God. Evangelistic agencies invade slums and prisons to bring prodigals back from the far country. But the Bible school invades the hopeful field of child nature and claims it for Jesus Christ's triumphal chariot. It seeks to bring the spirit of childhood to the one qualified Saviour and the one rightful King. God proposes the conquest of youth and every one active in this field is a partner with God in this business. Would that every Christian pastor, father, mother and teacher might think of themselves as constituting God's battalions to capture citadels of youth for the only and qualified Saviour and Lord of men, Jesus Christ.

Partners with God means in business with God. Surely the Eternal God is the senior Partner. He understands the business better than anyone. He knows what is needed. His resources are mighty.

Partners with God. This lifts the lowliest Christian work to a high plane of honor, dignity, privilege and responsibility. God is in it, back of it, and for it. He means to pursue it with us, to make it pay dividends in lives redeemed, built up, empowered and guided.

Partners with God. His is the kingdom, the power and the glory. We are dependent; we are at best channels of blessing, instruments, agents, witnesses, ambassadors, salt and light to a world which needs Jesus.

Partners with God. You can expect success. Christ can never fail. Victory is sure. Deal only in God's Word and it shall not return void.

Partners with God. He will value it and reward it. The business done for God is the thing which will last. It is the one thing you will be glad to have associated with your name. It will prove to have been life's greatest honor.

Partners with God. We read concerning the disciples after the risen Christ sat down at the right hand of God, "And they went forth, and preached everywhere, the Lord working with them, and confirming the word by the signs that followed." The Lord of glory never forsakes those who are engaged in His business. He never leaves them to work alone. He works too. He honors faith and devotion. He sees to results and causes us to see that our labor is not in vain in the Lord.

Partners with God. The spirit that crucified Jesus is still in the world. It opposes the worker and seeks to destroy the work now as always. But God will show the world the futility of fighting Him. "He that sitteth in the heavens will laugh: The Lord will have them in derision." Meanwhile, it must be remembered that the servant is not greater than his Lord. Our missionaries in Japan and China, for example, are already sharing in a new way in the suffering of Christ. Their families are scattered perhaps, and brave men and women continue on the firing line for God, exposed to the horrors of modern warfare. Soldiers of the cross are they, good soldiers of Jesus Christ and partners with God in costly and Christlike sacrifice. Surely, from every Christian home in America the cry of intercessory prayer will rise that they and we may be true partners with God, bent on God's business, not closing down and retiring, but doing what Christ would do and wants done. Now is a time for the martyr spirit, the true warrior spirit, the setting of the face steadfastly toward those strongholds of Satan where crosses loom for those who would follow in Christ's train.

Partners with God. Each and every one of us must see how the song fits, "I'm here on business for the King."

Sources of Christian Joy

THE PROMISED LAND

There is a promised land
  Within the reach of all;
To enter needs but faith
  In answer to Christ's call.
No dim and distant goal
  Of human striving this;
It lies within the soul,
  A state of inner bliss.

It is the death of self,
  A life made new in Christ,
A blest experience
  Of peace and joy unpriced;
It is the reign of love,
  A kingdom of good-will
In souls by Christ inspired
  His mission to fulfil.

There is a promised land
  Before the church of God,
Where faith and purpose blend
  To tell His love abroad;
A state of conscious power,
  A sense of joy divine
In tasks assumed and done
  To make His glory shine.

There is a promised land
  For nations to attain,
If they in tune with Christ
  Their selfishness restrain;
An era of sweet peace,
  Of acted brotherhood,
Where all compete to seek
  The universal good.

13

SOURCES OF CHRISTIAN JOY

A child of God should be a visible beatitude for joy and happiness, and a living doxology for gratitude and adoration. —SPURGEON

CHRISTIAN PEOPLE share in all the ills flesh is heir to. It often seems as if they have more than their share of misfortune and sorrow. It is not now our purpose to discuss the reasons for this. God's people have many sources of joy even in the midst of affliction.

There is the joy of the forgiveness of sins, of being right with God, of having peace through the blood of the cross. The consciousness of unforgiven sin is a real barrier to joy. John Bunyan tells us in his *Grace Abounding* of the struggle he had with the fear that he had committed the unpardonable sin. He suffered prolonged torment on this account. But at last he came to the light and was able unreservedly to trust in Christ's redeeming blood. Then followed raptures of joy such as only those experience who bring their load of guilt to the Lord and find that He bears it away. And numbers of hymns express the joy that is felt when Christ has been received as a personal Saviour. So great is the joy that it voices itself in song and makes life radiant.

We mention also the joy of overcoming, of moral and spiritual victory. The allurements of the world offer present and tangible satisfactions and the reason they are so often effective in gaining acceptance is the prospect of immediate pleasure. But they leave a nasty taste. They rob life of true joy. If purchased at the price of conscience and in defiance of the known will of God, their end is bitterness to those seduced thereby. He who consults the will of God and defers to it reaps a deep and abiding joy for the sinful pleasures he denies himself. It is ever true that to do a mean thing makes one feel mean. Any temptation resisted adds to solid happiness. Whenever we score a victory for God in our personal lives, we are thrilled with heavenly joy.

Another source of Christian joy is the consciousness of being on the winning side. The great battle of the ages is the conflict between righteousness and sin. A man may steep his life in unholy pleasures, but his own conscience will bear him witness that "the wages of sin is death." A man cannot hold out against God forever and look forward to winning out in the game of life. "Christ hath conquered every foe" and as Christians the assured victory of the Kingdom is a fountain of precious joy. However dark the outlook for righteousness may be at any given moment, we live in a moral universe and God overrules every passion of men for the ends of the Kingdom.

It is a joy to win souls for Christ and to serve humanity in the name of Christ. Selfishness is not a way of happiness. The true joy of life lies beneath the load of our fellows. When we bear one another's burdens, it puts a song in our own hearts. Nothing is more productive of genuine bliss than to lead the sin-laden to the merciful Saviour. Sweet has been the spiritual rapture of soul-winners. The joy in heaven over one sinner that repenteth is shared by those who put the sinner in saving touch with Christ.

There is the joy of communion with God through believing prayer. When Jesus prayed on the mount, He was transfigured before His intimates. So prayer always works transformingly and our unselfish intercession for others brings music into our own souls. Prayer begets praise because it fills the heart with gladness. Those who take no time for the secret place miss a deep fountain of divine joy. Life is so hurried today that many feel they have no time for prayer. No mistake could be more tragic. Life at its best is sustained by prayer. God is the source of every true delight and His presence becomes a reality through prayer.

Also, we mention the joy of sufficient grace for every need, the joy of always being sufficient in all things. God has given us exceeding great and precious promises for every step of the way. His presence never fails. Strength for daily need comes to every waiting and believing soul. To know that no trial can ever come for which God has not provided the necessary spiritual resources is indeed a joy.

Why, then, should we not enjoy our rich inheritance? It lies about us on every hand. God has done all. There is no limit to our possibilities in the Christian life. "Onward and upward" is the watchword. "For everyone that asketh receiveth; and he that seeketh findeth; and to him that knocketh it shall be opened."